7

Murder in Play

A play

Simon Brett

Samuel French — London
New York — Toronto — Hollywood

ISBN 0 573 01840 5

Please see page iv for further copyright information.

MURDER IN PLAY

Commissioned by Richard Cohen for the 1993 Cheltenham Festival of Literature and first produced, under the title *Dead Bodies Everywhere*, in the Shaftesbury Hall Theatre, Cheltenham, on 10th October, 1993, with the following cast (all members of Cheltenham College):

Renee Savage	Anna Sanford
Tim Fermor	Giles Major
Ginette Vincent	Leah Smith
Christa d'Amato	Anna Heywood
Sophie Lawton	Emily Peck
Harrison Bracewell	Paul Rose
Boris Smolensky	Ben Shore
Pat	Anneli Oakes

Directed by **Chris Haslam**, **Antony Lyons** and **Kerstin Jarman**
Designed by **Mark Johnstone**

The action of the play takes place in the Library of Priorswell Manor

MURDER AT PRIORSWELL MANOR

Cast (in order of their appearance):

Lady Dorothy Cholmondley — *Renee*
Major Rodney Pirbright — *Tim*
Lady Virginia Cholmondley — *Ginette*
Mrs Puttock — *Christa*
Triggs ————— *Sophie*
Mr Papadopoulos ——— *Sophie*
Boris Smolensky — *Harrison*
Pat
Inspector ——— *Harrison*

ACT I   A summer afternoon

       Interval

ACT II   Scene 1   Six days later
       Scene 2   The following day

Your programme for the play will probably list the casting for *Murder At Priorswell Manor*, in order to suspend the audience's disbelief until the play-within-a-play formula is revealed.

DRAMATIS PERSONAE OF *MURDER IN PLAY*

—as opposed to the dramatis personae of *Murder At Priorswell Manor*, the deathless stage thriller which they are currently dress-rehearsing.

Lady Dorothy Cholmondley is played by **Renee Savage**, a classically-trained actress in her—let's be generous—late forties. She is the wife of the theatre's director, Boris Smolensky, and tends—surprise, surprise—to get leading roles in a lot of his productions.

Boris himself is more than a bit of a poseur. He has spoken with a Russian accent for so long that no one ever questions whether he really is Russian or not. He is one of those directors who is hooked on power and his ego is enormous. He thinks his productions are the most brilliant ever devised and cannot understand why the world of international theatre does not share this view. He also cannot imagine the existence of a woman who does not find him physically irresistible. Boris is younger than his wife, but not as young as the tight denim, cowboy boots and ponytail he affects.

Major Rodney Pirbright is played by **Tim Fermor**, a slightly petulant, self-obsessed actor in his early thirties; and Virginia Cholmondley by **Ginette Vincent**, extremely young, extremely pretty, and extremely brainless.

The actress playing Mrs Puttock is **Christa d'Amato**. She is in her fifties and, as she tells everyone within seconds of meeting, used to be one of the regular characters in the television soap opera, *Harley's Hotel*.

Triggs is played by **Sophie Lawton**, an intelligent and attractive actress in her late twenties.

The part of Mr Papadopoulos is taken by **Harrison Bracewell**, in his sixties and an actor of the old school. He has a bit of a drink problem and is not great about remembering lines. He claims to know everyone in "the business" and, when given the chance—which is rarely—likes to relate anecdotes of all the stars he's worked with.

The final component of the production team for *Murder at Priorswell Manor* is Boris's regular Stage Manager, Pat. She is not particularly attractive and her permanent uniform of paint-spattered t-shirt, jeans and trainers doesn't add much to her physical charms.

In the extracts from the play-within-the-play, the cast are given the names of the characters in that play. For the rest of the action, they are given their real names.

ACT I

The setting throughout is the Library of Priorswell Manor. This is represented by a rather shabby-looking box-set. If the scenery has the feeling of any specific time, it is the early thirties

CS *is a large fireplace, on the wall above which hangs a spray of swords, pikes, etc., covered at their conjunction by a metal shield. To the left of the fireplace stands a drinks trolley, with an array of bottles, decanters, soda siphons etc. Next to this are french windows, too closely behind which hangs a less-than-convincing backdrop of extensive gardens. On the other side of the fireplace, R, stands a large cupboard, the size of a wardrobe. Against the wall, DL of the french windows, is a locked desk. Doors in the downstage flats on each side lead offstage, but there are also possible entrances between the edges of the set and the proscenium arch. Facing front in the centre of the acting area are a chaise-longue and two high-backed armchairs. By the chaise-longue stands a small drinks table*

On the walls hang a few rather non-descript paintings of obscure Cholmondley ancestors and stags at bay. Though the room is designated "The Library", there are very few books in evidence

The impression of the whole set is that it comes from a cost-conscious repertory production of a stage thriller at almost any time during the last forty years

As the action opens, it is late afternoon. The interior lights—standard lamp, etc.—are on, though the general lighting has a rather stagey feel

Lady Dorothy Cholmondley, a dowager in her sixties, is seated on the chaise-longue. She wears an evening dress appropriate to her station. Triggs, in neat housemaid's uniform with a very small white apron, stands at the back of the stage by the drinks table. Major Rodney Pirbright, about thirty, wearing a military dinner jacket; and Virginia Cholmondley, an ingenue in evening dress, stand rather awkwardly downstage. The period of their costumes is approximately between-the-wars. Lady Dorothy and Virginia have empty sherry glasses, Rodney a whisky and soda

All the characters act in a slightly stilted way, so that it's difficult for the audience to tell whether they're doing it deliberately or are just bad actors. With Virginia, however, there's no doubt. She is a very bad actress

Lady Dorothy I am surprised that Mr Papadopoulos has not joined us for a preprandial drink. The gong will be sounding soon, and he's always seemed so very dependent on his whisky and soda.

Rodney Typical, if I may say, of the way the bounder embraces all things British, that whisky and soda. No doubt, where he comes from, he'd be raising a glass of kumquat, arak or some other infernal distillation.

Lady Dorothy Please, Major Pirbright. It is inappropriate to speak in that manner of another gentleman.

Rodney And I can assure you I would not, Lady Cholmondley, if Mr Papadopoulos *were* a gentleman.

Lady Dorothy Whatever his breeding—or lack of it, Major Pirbright—he is my guest here at Priorswell Manor.

Virginia Yes, Mummy, but that's only because Daddy's will left you so strapped for cash that—

Lady Dorothy Virginia! To speak of money in mixed society is the hallmark of inadequate breeding.

Virginia Sorry, Mummy. But Mr Papadopoulos speaks of money all the time.

Rodney Which rather proves my point, I would have said. The swarthy dago's an absolute bounder.

Lady Dorothy Major Pirbright, in my experience, a detached gentility and sympathy is the appropriate mode of behaviour when dealing with those so unfortunate as not to be British.

Rodney Regrettably, Lady Cholmondley, such an approach all too often proves inadequate. The only language a thimblerigger like Papadopoulos understands is the language of the horsewhip. And I certainly wouldn't be ashamed to take one to the cad.

Virginia Oh, Rodney, you're so brave.

Mrs Puttock enters in distress, from the door L. In her fifties, she is the cook/housekeeper and dressed accordingly in a full-length black dress and long apron. She speaks in stage Cockney

Mrs Puttock Oh, milady, milady!

Lady Dorothy What is it, Mrs Puttock? It must be something of considerable importance to justify the irruption of a cook/housekeeper into the library when my weekend houseguests are enjoying their preprandial drinks.

Mrs Puttock It is of great importance. It's the carving knife, milady!

Lady Dorothy What about the carving knife?

Mrs Puttock It's gorn missing!

Lady Dorothy Gorn missing?

Mrs Puttock Yes, milady. And just after Sergeant Bovis from the village police station called to warn us there's an escaped prisoner on the loose.

Virginia An escaped prisoner—oh, how too ghastly!

Rodney Don't worry yourself, my angel. I'll be here to protect you.

Lady Dorothy gives him a quizzical look

And you of course, Lady Cholmondley. Tell me, Mrs Puttock, for what crime was this escaped prisoner incarcerated?

Mrs Puttock (*dramatically*) Murder, Major Pirbright. Murder by stabbing.

Rodney Huh. (*He draws his service revolver from his trouser pocket*) Well, just let him try any of his little schemes at Priorswell Manor. He'll find that Major Rodney Pirbright is more than ready for him.

Lady Dorothy Major Pirbright, where did you get that gun?

Rodney From the war, Lady Cholmondley. (*His face goes into involuntary spasm*) Mind you, it wasn't the only thing I got from the war.

Virginia Rodney, please! You must just try to forget about your shell-shock.

Rodney (*nobly*) Yes, yes, my love. Sorry. Still, I'll just take a shufti in the garden. (*He moves across to open the french windows. They are jammed and it takes him a couple of attempts to get them open*) Best to be sure we're safe when there are ladies in the house.

Virginia Oh, Rodney, you are brave.

Mrs Puttock (*sobbing*) Milady, I'm so frightened.

Lady Dorothy Pull yourself together, Mrs Puttock, don't be ridiculous. Triggs, my guests and I require more drinks. And, Mrs Puttock, go back to the kitchen and pour yourself a large glass of cooking sherry.

Triggs, who has been standing rather bored at the back of the set, comes to life. She moves forward, carrying an empty decanter of sherry, and mimes refilling Lady Dorothy's glass. Mrs Puttock curtsys and makes as if to exit left, until she is stopped by Rodney's words

Rodney (*looking offstage and continuing over Trigg's actions*) By thunder, I think I see movement in the shrubbery!

Virginia Oh, don't shoot, Rodney! You know I can't stand bangs!

Rodney Sorry, my love, but you keep out of this. It's man's work. (*He takes aim carefully*) And when the work required is shooting some confounded malefactor, Major Rodney Pirbright's not the man to shirk it! Right, take that, you delinquent scum!

Rodney pulls the trigger of his revolver, and is clearly surprised that it doesn't fire. The other characters look slightly uneasy. Rodney himself is fazed for a second, then improvises a line

You're facing one of the most deadly and infallible weapons in the world . . . (*He pulls the trigger again. Nothing happens. He pulls it a third time. There is silence, but he recoils as if the gun's gone off*) . . . with a very sophisticated silencer. (*He peers out into the garden*) I think I at least winged the rotter.

He moves back into the room. The other characters look expectantly towards the french windows. Lady Dorothy mimes gulping down her glass of sherry. There is a pause

Mr Papadopoulos totters in through the french windows, gasping and spluttering. He looks very foreign and wears an obvious wig. He is dressed in a rather flamboyant dinner suit with a jewelled insignia on a sash across his ample frontage. On his shirtfront is a wet splash of red. He sways in the middle of the stage

Virginia Mr Papadopoulos!

Mr Papadopoulos (*gasping feebly and dramatically in a very thick foreign accent*) I've . . . been . . . murdered!

He falls forward, face down. When he is on the ground the audience can see the handle of a carving knife sticking out of his back. The cast form an appalled circle around him. They hold the tableau. For too long. The silence becomes awkwardly long. But still they do not move

Boris's Voice (*in a Russian accent, heard on tannoy distort from the back of the auditorium*) And . . . curtain. End of Act One.

The lighting changes abruptly. The stage and a small area to the front of the auditorium are lit by bright working lights. The cast relax and drop out of character. They look vaguely up towards a real or imagined control box at the back of the auditorium

That was terrible! Terrible! You've forgotten all the notes I gave you. It's back to how it was on the first readthrough and the bloody play's opening tomorrow night! I'll be right down!

As soon as Boris finishes speaking the cast start chattering. Some slump into chairs—it's been a long rehearsal

Pat comes in from the wings with a hammer and Stanley knife and, oblivious to all that's going on around her, tries to find out why the french windows jammed

The cast form little huddles and their conversations overlap

Tim God, I thought I'd die when the gun wouldn't go off.
Christa (*sarcastically*) Still, what quick thinking. That silencer line was very clever, Tim. Very clever indeed.
Harrison (*over the end of this, picking himself up off the floor*) Actually, I heard a very good story about what Ralph (*pronounced "Rafe"*) Richardson once did when a gun wouldn't go off in—
Renee (*rounding on him in fury*) Now listen, Harrison, if you ever dare to upstage me again like you did on my entrance from the garden, I'll murder you.
Harrison I didn't deliberately upstage you, old girl.
Renee I am not an old girl!
Christa (*in a deliberately audible whisper*) Matter of opinion, I'd've said.

Renee gives her a furious look, but doesn't rise to the gibe

Harrison No, honestly, Renee love, it's that cupboard. I couldn't—
Renee (*ignoring him and steaming past to vent further spleen on Pat*) And, Pat, why in God's name wasn't there any sherry in the decanter? How the hell am I supposed to act when I haven't even got the right props?
Pat Look, I'm sorry, there was a lot to do when I reset the stage. It'll be there on the night, I promise.
Renee On the night is not good enough. I needed it there for the run.
Harrison (*who has been trying, without much success, to extract the carving knife out of his back*) I say, could someone give me a hand with this?

Sophie (*coming across to help him*) Sure. Can't have you walking around all day doing doner kebab impressions, can we?
Harrison Bless you, Sophie love.

She tries to remove the knife from his back

Lovely performance you're giving as Triggs, incidentally—very true.
Sophie Thank you, Harry. And of course it gets better.
Harrison Oh?
Sophie In Act Two Triggs has a line. (*In a housemaid voice and doing a little curtsy*) "Yes, milady." Huh—three years at drama school for that. (*She removes the knife*) There.
Harrison Thanks, darling.

Sophie moves away across the stage. Harrison, removing his wig, does not notice she's gone

Funny when Tim's gun wouldn't go off, wasn't it? Reminds me of a story Ralph Richardson once told me when I was working with him. He was in some dreadful stage thriller apparently and had to be shot at the end of the first act and—(*He looks round and realises that he's talking to himself, so stops*)

Sophie is near Ginette, who is sitting on the edge of the stage

Ginette You don't think I'm playing Virginia too stupid, do you, Sophie?
Sophie What? No, no, you're fine.
Ginette It is difficult playing someone stupid, you know.
Renee Don't worry, Ginette dear. You're doing it as if to the manner born.

Sophie nearly lets out a guilty giggle at this, but Ginetee is too stupid even to be aware of the implied insult. Tim homes in on Ginette. Sophie drifts away

Tim I thought your performance was great, Ginette.
Ginette (*slightly awkwardly*) Thank you.
Tim Nobody'd know it was your first acting job.
Ginette Oh. Good.
Tim (*sitting on the stage beside her*) Listen, Ginette, we've got to talk.
Ginette I don't think we've got much to talk about, Tim.
Tim But we have. We—

Boris enters from the back of the auditorium carrying a clipboard covered in notes

Boris (*shouting volubly*) That was dreadful! You've forgotten everything I've told you!

Boris comes storming towards the stage. Tim moves huffily away from Ginette

(*Approaching the stage*) What are you all playing at, for God's sake? You were terrible!

Boris is now right by Ginette, who is looking at him rather plaintively. Boris checks that Renee has her back to him, then touches Ginette's cheek

(*Softly*) With a few exceptions.

Ginette (*simpering*) Thank you, Boris.

Boris (*bouncing up on to the stage*) Right, gather round and let's see if we can salvage anything from this total fiasco!

Renee (*coming towards him*) Fiasco is right. I mean, how on earth I'm expected to begin to give a performance when I haven't got the right props, I just can't imagine.

Boris (*giving her a little pat on the shoulder*) Don't worry, love. We'll get it sorted. (*Bawling out*) Pat, why the hell wasn't there any sherry in that decanter?

Pat It just got missed. Won't happen again.

Boris Better bloody not happen again. Do you all realise that "Murder at Priorswell Manor" opens tomorrow night? I mean, come *on*.

Christa I'm fully aware that "Murder at Priorswell Manor" opens tomorrow night, Boris. That's why I'm still holding something back.

Renee (*with a patronising smile*) Must be nice to be able to do that. I'm the sort of actress who never holds anything back.

Christa (*with a sweet smile*) Except younger and more talented actresses, eh?

Renee looks at her balefully

Boris Anyway, come on, I want more from all of you. Where's the life? Where's the energy?

Tim The energy went about three hours ago. Look, we started at nine this morning and it's taken us five hours to get to the end of Act One.

Boris And it may take us another ten hours to get to the end of the play, but at least we'll get it right.

Tim We certainly won't be doing another ten hours, Boris.

Boris What do you mean?

Tim There are Equity regulations about the number of hours actors can work—

Boris Oh, for heaven's sake, Tim! If you wanted to spend your life clock-watching, you should have gone into the Civil Service, not the theatre.

Tim The fact remains—

Boris (*consulting his clipboard*) Quiet, please. I am giving notes. The gun. Major Pirbright's gun—what on earth happened with it?

Sophie It didn't go off.

Boris I could *see* it didn't go off, Sophie. I am asking *why* it didn't go off.

Harrison Actually, there's a rather funny story about what happened when Ralph Richardson was in a—

Boris We don't want any funny stories. Come on, who's responsible for the gun? *Pat*, why didn't you get us a gun that worked, for heaven's sake?

Pat (*as ever, not rising to his rudeness*) It did work at previous rehearsals.

Boris Where did you get it from?

Harrison It's mine. Belonged to my father. Found it after the old boy'd popped his clogs. With lots of live ammo and a box of blanks. Maybe the pin got stuck. Think that's what Ralph Richardson said happened when he was—

Boris Well, have a look at the gun and *get the bloody thing working!*

Harrison All right.

Tim hands the gun across to Harrison, who starts inspecting it

Boris Next thing . . . (*consulting his clipboard*) Sophie, your Triggs is looking bored.

Sophie Yes.

Boris Why?

Sophie Well, because she is bored. She's been standing by the drinks trolley not saying anything for half an hour. Wouldn't you look bored?

Boris She needs to be more animated.

Sophie More animated? Am I allowed to move?

Boris No, of course not.

Sophie Am I allowed to make faces?

Boris No.

Sophie Can't move, can't make faces, but I've still got to make her look animated?

Boris Yes.

Sophie (*with irony*) I see. Fine.

Boris (*turning back to his clipboard*) Now . . . what was next . . .? Oh yes, right at the end of the Act One—

Harrison, who has been checking the gun through this, looks along the barrel. It is pointing at Boris's back, though Harrison is not particularly aware of this. He pulls the trigger. There is a loud bang. Boris, interrupted in mid-speech, leaps out of his skin, and all the others on stage react

What the hell?!

Harrison (*with satisfaction*) Well, at least I got it working. That was a blank, incidentally.

Boris How do you know?

Sophie Because, if it hadn't been, Boris, you'd be dead.

Boris Hm. Yes. Well, be careful with it, Harrison. No waving the thing around when you're drunk, OK?

Harrison I've given up drinking, Boris.

Boris And you'd better not start again. Remember—if I find another bottle in your dressing room, you'll be out of this production.

Harrison All right, all right.

Boris Now where was I . . .? (*He consults his clipboard and sees something he doesn't understand*) "Bloody" . . .?

Christa Bloody what?

Boris Bloody . . .? (*Remembering why he'd made the note*) Oh yes, bloody *blood*. Harrison—your blood.

Harrison What about it?

Boris Not enough.

Harrison Not enough?

Boris No, not nearly enough. Look, this is the end of the act—the end of Act One. I want the audience to go out at the interval shocked because they've just seen a bloody murder—and I mean bloody. Harrison, I want you to look like an accident in an abattoir.

Harrison Oh. More blood then?

Boris Of course more blood! (*He looks back at his clipboard*) Now . . .

Renee Boris love, we really must do some work on that bit where I come in through the french windows with the carving knife. I mean, it's one of the climaxes of Act One and at the moment it's going for nothing because Harrison's mugging away like . . .

Boris Yes, yes, my love, we'd better look at that immediately.

Tim Listen, you can't just work straight through.

Boris Why not?

Tim Because we all need a break.

Boris We don't need a break. We need this play to open tomorrow night.

Tim I'm Equity representative in this company and the regulations clearly state that we should have had a lunch break an hour ago.

The cast react enthusiastically to the idea

Boris But . . . (*He realises he's up against all of them*) All right. Half an hour.

Tim Should be an hour.

Boris Half an hour from . . . (*he looks at his watch and claps his hands*) . . . now!

Pat, Harrison, Tim and Sophie, with some relief, move off through the DL *exit or the french windows—which Pat has now fixed—towards the Green Room*

Renee drapes herself over the chaise-longue

Christa (*to Renee*) You not having anything to eat?

Renee I don't do lunch.

Christa You should. You should look after your body . . . particularly as you get older.

Renee What, stuff it full of that health food muck, like you do?

Christa Don't knock it. I'll bet I live longer than you do, Renee.

Renee If you call subsisting on squashed vegetables living.

Christa Huh. (*Moving off* R) I'm going to liquidize my lunch.

Renee Thanks for the warning, Christa. I'll keep out of the dressing room till that pondweed smell dies down.

Christa exits huffily R

While this exchange has been going on, Boris has remained, consulting his clipboard and script. Ginette has waited at the side of the stage, hoping Boris will turn towards her. However, he looks up from his clipboard and moves across towards Renee

Disappointed, Ginette moves towards the exit. Harrison, who has continued inspecting the mechanism of his revolver, sees her going and moves across to join her

Harrison (*as they go out*) Ginette my dear, I think you might be amused by this story Ralph Richardson once told me. He was acting in this dire thriller in some tin-pot weekly rep when . . .

Boris (*looking down at Renee*) Are you all right, my love?

Renee (*reaching up to take his hand*) Oh yes, you know, just tired.

Boris Sure it's not . . .?

Renee No, no. Just the odd twinge.

Boris Hm.

Renee (*releasing his hand*) I do know about you and Ginette, Boris.

Boris Ah.

Renee I always know. You're very transparent.

Boris Am I?

Renee Oh yes. Very transparent and, from my point of view, very safe.

Boris What do you mean by that?

Renee I mean that you'd never actually leave me. Oh, you'll go off doing naughties with some little actress in her digs . . . Where is it this one's staying? Nice little farmhouse, isn't it? Must be so convenient. All those cows . . . nice for Ginette to have someone of her own intelligence to talk to.

Boris Renee . . .

Renee But I don't mind about all that. It doesn't worry me. I know you'll never actually leave. You like your home comforts too much. Beneath your flamboyantly Bohemian exterior, Boris Smolensky, you're really rather an ordinary, conventional, boring little man.

Boris Am I? I might surprise you one day, Renee.

Renee (*with a little laugh*) Has to be a first time.

Christa comes on stage during the end of this exchange. She wears modern glasses and carries a creamy-looking greenish drink in a Tupperware container. She clears her throat

Christa Sorry. Hope I'm not disturbing anything.

Boris No, no, I was just going to give the others some notes.

Boris walks briskly off L, looking at his clipboard

Christa sits on one of the armchairs near Renee, takes the lid off her Tupperware container and starts to drink the creamy green fluid

Renee What on earth is it this time?

Christa Spinach, orange, lemon, nettles and garlic . . . mostly.

Renee Good God.

Christa This stuff's absolutely marvellous. Why do you think it is, Renee, that when I look in my mirror I see the skin of a twenty-year-old?

Renee Perhaps because you're short-sighted . . .?

Christa (*with a sweet smile*) Maybe you should try some of this, Renee dear . . .? Undo some of the ravages, eh?

Renee does not think this worthy of response. Besides, she is really feeling too tired for a fight

I'll have you know, this drink is what kept me going when I was doing "Harley's Hotel." Week in, week out, all those long sessions in the studio . . . I'd have one of these twice a day . . . and I could just go on for ever.

Renee (*unable to resist the comeback*) Hm. Pity the series didn't.

Christa (*stung*) Television planners never have had any taste. You know, even now, three years after it finished, I'm still getting a huge postbag from people whose lives just aren't the same without "Harley's Hotel". (*Pause*) Pity your television career never took off, wasn't it, Renee?

Renee (*annoyed in spite of herself*) I never wanted it to take off. The theatre has always been my first love. I'm very happy with the situation as it is.

Christa Not surprised. Perfect for you, I'd have thought. When your husband's the Artistic Director and gives you all the leading roles . . .

Renee Christa . . .

Christa Even those you're just the teensiest bit too old for.

Renee I can assure you Boris has never cast me in any part for which I was not the best available candidate. You may not know this, Christa, but when I came out of RADA, I was top of my year.

Christa Really?

Renee People still talk about Renee Savage's Cleopatra.

Christa Oh, I'm sure they do, dear . . . but what do they *say*?

Renee All the critics agreed I was destined to go right to the top.

Christa What went wrong then?

Renee Wrong?

Christa Well, I mean, would you really describe hogging all the leads in a tatty touring company as "the top"?

Renee I do not "hog all the leads"! No, the fact is . . . my career went . . . Well, I had problems with my health.

Christa Oh yes. Actresses are so prone to have problems with their health . . . particularly, I find, when they've just failed auditions for major parts.

Renee Christa, I really haven't the energy to respond to all your bitching.

Christa No, well, I'm sure you're very tired. Looking after Boris must be a full-time occupation. Not, I imagine, from the sex point of view, though. His casting couch is pretty mobile these days, isn't it?

Renee Christa, I am fully aware of all Boris's little adventures.

Christa Oh, good. I've been keeping an eye on him too. (*Sweetly*) We must check our lists at some point, mustn't we, and make sure you haven't missed any.

Renee gives Christa a little smile, before moving on to a new tack

Renee Funny, isn't it, that since "Harley's Hotel" finished, you haven't been offered *any* other television work . . .? Still, I suppose the public memory is very short, isn't it?

Christa I'll have you know, the public still remembers me very well indeed. That's why I was asked to join this campaign . . . you know, "Values and Morality in Television".

Renee Oh yes. VOMIT.

Christa It's called VAMIT.

Renee Well, I know what you mean, dear, anyway.

Christa They asked me to join because they want famous names to raise their profile. I certainly haven't been forgotten, Renee. I've never been less than a star—from the moment I started in the business.

Renee Oh. Actually, I wanted to talk to you about that, Christa. I found out something rather fascinating about your early days.

Christa About my early days?

Renee Yes. Something that might well interest the "Harley's Hotel" fan magazine if—

She is interrupted by the entrance from the wings of Pat, carrying a portable phone

Pat Call for you, Christa.

Christa Oh. Is it the agent?

Pat No. Someone from . . . I think they said VOMIT.

Renee smiles

Christa V*A*MIT. (*Taking the phone from Pat and moving out to the wings*) I'll take it somewhere a bit more private.

Pat You can use the office phone. That's only the extension.

Christa Right. (*Into the phone as she goes*) Hell-o. Just moving to another phone if you could bear with me . . .

Christa exits

Pat is about to follow her off

Boris and Harrison enter L. *Boris still carries his clipboard, and Harrison holds a sandwich. The old actor is once again trying to tell his Ralph Richardson story*

Harrison . . . and, anyway, the thing is, Ralph Richardson was in this dreadful—

Boris Pat, we must look at that cupboard.

Harrison starts eating his sandwich

Pat (*moving across to the cupboard*) OK.

Renee (*from her chaise-longue*) Yes, we don't want a repetition of what happened on the run, with the door opening at just the wrong moment.

Boris (*opening the cupboard doors and looking at them*) No, we don't. For heaven's sake, Pat you idiot, why couldn't you get a cupboard with doors that stayed closed?

Pat With the budget you gave me, I was lucky to get any kind of cupboard. (*Closing the doors and opening them again*) Maybe I can fix a catch on the inside . . .?

Boris Yes, do that.

Pat gets inside the cupboard to inspect the problem

Do anything—so long as you make the bloody things work!

Boris studies his clipboard. Renee has found a magazine on the set and is reading it in a desultory manner. There is silence. Harrison sees an opportunity to tell his story

Harrison Anyway, what happened was, Ralph Richardson was touring in this dreadful thriller, and there was a moment in it when he was meant to shoot another character. He pulled the trigger on the gun—bugger-all happened. He tried again—no dice. Knew he had to do something, couldn't think what, so he just moved forward and gave his supposed victim a great kick up the bum. Other actor staggered downstage, clutching his hindquarters and dropped to the ground gasping, "The boot . . . The boot was poisoned!"

He roars with laughter and looks round for reaction from the others. Nothing—none of them has heard the joke. Disconsolately, Harrison takes another bite from his sandwich

Pat (*coming out of the cupboard*) Yes, I can fix it. (*Moving off towards the exit* L) There's a spring catch in the Props Room.
Boris Well, just make sure it bloody well works!
Pat (*impervious to his rudeness*) Yes, yes, Boris.

Pat exits

Boris (*calling after her*) . . . because we won't have time to rehearse it again before tomorrow night.
Renee (*very casual*) Excuse me, darling . . .
Boris (*looking back at his clipboard*) Hm?
Renee We will have time to rehearse it again before tomorrow night.
Boris Sorry, love. I've got a hell of a tight schedule and—
Renee (*quiet but steely*) Boris, we *will* have time to rehearse it again before tomorrow night.
Boris (*caving in immediately*) Oh, all right, love. Sure I'll manage to fit it in. In fact, we'll do it first thing after the break. Harrison . . .
Harrison Mm?
Boris Straight after the break—we'll do your Mr Papadopoulos in the cupboard bit.
Harrison Right-ho.
Boris Assuming we've got a catch on it by then. (*Bawling off left*) Pat, hurry along with fixing that flaming cupboard, will you! (*Consulting his clipboard and hurrying* L) Oh, I must talk to Tim about his facial tic. It's meant to look like shell-shock, not a bloody orgasm.

Boris exits

*Harrison sits in an armchair and continues eating his sandwich. There is
a silence*

Renee I wouldn't advise you to try upstaging me, Harrison.
Harrison I wasn't. I didn't.
Renee Huh.
Harrison Actually, there was rather a good story about upstaging
    when I was working with Johnnie at the Old Vic. He was—
Renee (*unaware of him, continuing on her own track*) No, acting's all
    about concentration . . . (*Intensely*) And I don't like people
    breaking breaking my concentration.
Harrison I won't do it. I promise.
Renee You'd better not. (*Casually*) I was wandering round backstage
    after rehearsal yesterday . . .
Harrison Oh?
Renee Went into your dressing room . . .
Harrison But why did—?
Renee (*over-riding him*) Not a very subtle place to hide a bottle of
    Scotch, is it—behind the radiator?
Harrison Renee . . . Renee, you won't tell Boris, will you?
Renee Depends a bit on how you behave, I'd say, Harry. Do I make
    myself clear?
Harrison Yes, Renee. Yes, very clear.
Renee (*easing herself up off the sofa*) Well, since nobody's brought me
    one, I suppose I'll have to go and get *myself* a cup of coffee.

   Renee trails languidly off L

*Harrison looks upset for a moment, then furtive. Checking offstage both
sides, he moves across to the fireplace. Reaching up to the display of
swords and pikes, he extracts a half-bottle of Scotch from behind the
shield. Looking round again, he unscrews it and takes a quick, but
substantial, swig. Hearing someone approach, he shoves the bottle back
behind the shield and moves nonchalantly downstage. As he does so, he
takes a packet of extra-strong mints out of his pocket and pops one into
his mouth*

   Pat enters L *with a tool box. Taking no notice of Harrison, she goes
   into the cupboard and starts fixing a catch on the inside of its doors*

   Tim and Sophie, carrying cups of coffee, come in

Harrison looks round to face them

Sophie You look frightfully guilty, Harry.

Tim Been raiding the Priorswell Manor drinks trolley, have you?

Harrison (*after a little laugh*) No, just having a sandwich. (*Crossing* L) Go and see if I can find another one, eh?

Harrison exits L

Tim and Sophie take no notice of Pat working away in the cupboard

Tim So . . . tomorrow night another tacky, cheapo-cheapo Boris Smolensky production will be under way.

Sophie Yes.

Tim (*bitterly*) If I could afford to, I'd get out of this tomorrow. The whole set-up's so tacky. It's typical of Boris that he's too mean even to get someone in to do the lights.

Sophie He says he does them himself because it gives us the feeling of an . . . (*going into an imitation of Boris's voice*) ensemble.

Tim Huh. An ensemble is meant to be about company spirit, whereas here . . . (*He shrugs with distaste, then becomes aware of Pat in the cupboard and lowers his voice*) I mean, Renee can't avoid staying— she's married to him and she gets all the good parts—but why on earth does Pat stick around? He's so rude to her all the time.

Sophie (*also in a low voice*) I imagine she's been working for Boris so long she just doesn't notice any more.

Tim Maybe. (*Back at normal volume, looking round at the set*) He's such a cheapskate, though.

Sophie Oh yes. If Boris Smolensky was producing *A Hundred and One Dalmatians*, it'd end up as "Spot the Dog."

Tim (*with a bitter laugh*) Too true. (*He shudders and sighs*) Oh God . . . the thought of three months of this . . .

Sophie (*sympathetically*) Yes, it must be particularly difficult for you.

Tim You have a gift for understatement, Sophie. Ginette and I came here as a unit. We were over the moon about working together . . . sorted out these nice digs out in a farmhouse and . . . Then, within the first week of rehearsals, bloody Boris'd come on to her and I was out.

Sophie I'm sorry. But does she really believe he's serious about her?

Tim Oh yes. In Ginette's scenario he's going to leave Renee and marry her.

In her cupboard at the back of the stage, Pat does a slight reaction to this

Oh, a lovely kid like that shouldn't be throwing herself away on some pretentious old has-been like Boris. Why do you think she does it?

Sophie Well . . . Well, part of the explanation may be that Ginette's not very bright, is she?

Tim (*affronted*) What do you mean—not very bright?

Sophie (*with a comprehending nod*) Ah. I see you're still in love with her, Tim.

Tim Yes, I am. And if Boris bloody Smolensky thinks he's going to get away with what he's done unpunished . . . well, he's got another think coming!

Ginette enters L. *She is carrying a plastic bottle full of a yellowish liquid. She stops when she sees Tim*

Ginette Oh. I was looking for Renee.

Sophie She was in the Green Room.

Ginette (*making as if to leave*) Well, maybe I'll—

Sophie (*moving tactfully to the entrance*) No, I'm just going to get more coffee. I'll tell Renee you're looking for her.

Sophie exits

Ginette stands awkwardly, wishing she'd thought quickly enough to get away. Tim rounds on her

Tim So . . . feeling good about yourself, are you?

Ginette What do you mean?

Tim Proud, are you, of messing up my life—and Renee's?

Ginette I haven't done anything against Renee.

Tim No?

Renee enters through the french windows unseen by Tim and Ginette. She holds a mug of coffee and stands in the doorway, listening to what is being said

Ginette No. Boris and Renee's marriage is over—in any real sense. These days she's only interested in her garden—well, and her acting, of course.

Tim Really? And who told you that?

Ginette (*innocently*) Boris.

Tim (*sarcastically*) Well, that *is* a surprise, isn't it?

Ginette Boris really wants me and Renee to be friends. And stay friends, you know, when . . .

Tim When what?

Ginette When he and I are together.

Tim For heaven's sake, Ginette! You mustn't believe all that bullshit he gives you. He tries the same line with every pretty little actress he works with . . . tells them all they've got star quality and their careers'll really take off . . . if they'll only go to bed with him. Surely you're not stupid enough to believe it?

Ginette looks at him resolutely

Well, perhaps you are. I'll tell you one thing, though. You stay with Boris and it'll be the end of your acting career. You'll just go on doing tatty productions like this for the rest of your days. Boris isn't going anywhere.

Ginette As a matter of fact, he is.

Tim What?

Ginette Boris's been offered another job.

Both Renee and Pat react to this news

In America.

Tim In America? Boris? You got to be joking.

Ginette No, it's true. At a theatre in New York. And when he goes, he's taking me with him.

Tim Don't be ridiculous! (*Suddenly putting his arms round her*) Listen, Ginette, I love you.

Ginette (*struggling to get free*) Let me go!

Tim Can't you understand that . . .?

Renee clears her throat loudly. Tim's words trickle away and he and Ginette draw apart

I must just . . . Something I've got to sort out.

Tim hurries awkwardly off L

Pat comes out of the cupboard and closes its doors. She seems satisfied with the result, and is about to go off L *when Renee, who is looking at the drinks trolley, interrupts her*

Renee You still haven't filled that decanter, Pat.

Pat (*picking up the empty decanter with a bad grace*) It's on my list.

Pat exits L

Renee, still carrying her coffee cup, moves languidly downstage to sit

once again on her chaise-longue. Ginette hovers awkwardly, holding her
plastic bottle. Renee looks up and gives her a patronising smile

Renee So . . .?

Ginette (*still awkward*) I brought something in for you.

Renee Oh?

Ginette (*proffering the bottle*) It's for the garden.

Renee The garden—of course. Yes, that's the only thing I care about,
isn't that right . . . now I've lost interest in sex?

Ginette Well . . . Boris said you'd been having problems with your
rosebeds . . .

Renee Did he? Boris presenting himself as worried about my
gardening problems—you really are getting the full charm
offensive, aren't you?

Ginette (*persevering*) . . . and I asked the farmer where I'm staying if
he knew anything good for—

Renee (*suddenly fierce*) Listen . . . Ginette—is that your name? I'm
sorry, there've been so many, I think I can be forgiven for mixing
you all up. I am fully aware of what's going on between you and
Boris.

Ginette Oh. And . . .?

Renee And nothing. I just hope you don't get hurt too much when he
drops you.

Ginette He's not going to drop me.

Renee Believe me, sweetie, he is. Other women to Boris are like
so many Kleenex. He picks them up, he snuffles around in them
for a little while, and then he drops them. All of them. They all
end up cast aside—on the ground—crumpled and covered with
snot.

Ginette It's different with Boris and me.

Renee No, it's not. And, you know, he always comes back to me in
the end. No other woman stands the remotest chance with Boris so
long as I'm alive.

Ginette (*doggedly*) Boris loves me. And we're going to America
together.

Renee (*infuriatingly soothing*) Of course, dear, of course you are.
How long have you had this problem with delusions? I've got the
name of a very good shrink, if you're interested.

Ginette You don't know anything about—

Renee (*fiercely*) I do know this. You won't keep him. The only way

you keep hold of a man like Boris is by putting him under lock and
key . . . unless of course you happen to be his wife.

Ginette But I'm going to be——

*Pat enters L with the filled decanter and goes across to place this on
the drinks trolley. Ginette, almost in tears, hurries across to exit L,
but is stopped by the arrival of the rest of the cast, led by Boris,
clapping his hands*

Boris OK, come on. Break over.

Tim We haven't had the full—

Boris Break over! Right, I want to pick it up just before Lady
Dorothy and Mrs Puttock's entrance from the garden.

Christa What's the line?

Boris My script's up in the lighting box. Pat, get the prompt copy.

Pat obediently exits L

Renee (*to Christa*) It's when we come in after Mr Papadopoulos has
hidden himself.

Christa Yes, but what's the actual line?

Renee Why, Christa dear, are you having difficulty remembering
them?

*Pat comes back with the open prompt copy, which she holds out to
Boris*

Christa No, of course I can bloody remember them! I'll have you
know, on "Harley's Hotel" there was a new half-hour script twice a
week to—

Boris We'll take it from the scene just before.

Sophie What, Triggs finding the carving knife?

Boris No, no. Rodney and Virginia on the sofa.

Sophie Right.

Sophie exits L

Ginette (*with an unenthusiastic look at Tim*) Do we have to do that
bit?

Boris Yes, yes. We need the run-in. (*Clapping his hands*) Now hurry,
hurry. We need Rodney and Virginia . . . and Mr Papadopoulos—
with Lady Dorothy and Mrs Puttock standing by—OK?

Tim and Ginette move towards the chaise-longue

Renee and Christa go out through the french windows

Harrison crosses to go out of the DR *door*

Boris Put your wig on, Harrison!
Harrison Oh yes. (*He grabs hold of it and puts it on*)
Tim (*feeling in his pocket*) Hey, I haven't got the gun. Who's got the gun?
Harrison I have. (*He takes it out of his pocket and gives it to him*) There.
Boris And you're sure it's working now?
Harrison Just checked it through.

Harrison exits through the DR *door and closes it after him*

Tim and Ginette, studiously ignoring each other, sit on the chaise-longue

Boris drops down off the stage into the auditorium

Boris OK. Take the lights as read. And start from . . . (*He consults Pat's prompt copy*) You, Ginette—"I'll help you to forget the past".
Ginette OK.
Pat (*from the edge of the stage*) Can I take the prompt copy?
Boris Mm. (*He hands it to her*)

Pat exits DL

"I'll help you to forget the past".
Ginette Now?
Boris Yes, now!

Tim and Ginette go into the style of "Murder at Priorswell Manor"

Virginia I'll help you to forget the past. Oh, Rodney, when we're married, I'll spend every minute of every day helping you to forget the past.
Rodney You make it sound so easy.
Virginia It will be easy. When we're married, we won't think about the past, because all our thoughts will be concentrated on the future. Rodney, I'll teach you to believe in the future. In a sunny, golden future for you and me.
Rodney Oh, I hope you can, my love. In my experience, whenever I dare think of a sunny, golden future, some hideous black cloud appears to shroud that splendid sun.

Mr Papadopoulos enters from the DR *door*

(*Standing*) Speak of the devil.

Mr Papadopoulos (*very smooth and unctuous*) I hope I am not quite so evil as the devil, Major Pirbright . . . (*He chuckles*) . . . though perhaps I am not all angel. (*He bows elaborately to Virginia*) Good afternoon, Lady Virginia. How beautiful you look, as ever. (*He takes her hand*) An English rose . . . ripe for plucking.

He bends to kiss her hand, but Rodney pushes him away

Rodney I'll thank you to keep your thick lips off my fiancée's hand.

Mr Papadopoulos (*with a shrug*) I am sorry. I merely follow the custom of my own country.

Rodney Well, you're not in your own country now. And nor am I—thank God!

Mr Papadopoulos No. You have never liked abroad, I think, Major Pirbright?

Rodney Deuced right I haven't. The only good things that ever came from abroad were curry, brandy and tobacco.

Mr Papadopoulos And, of course, your British Royal Family.

Rodney How dare you, you bounder!

Mr Papadopoulos But, in spite of claiming not to like abroad, you have spent quite a lot of time there, haven't you, Major Pirbright?

Rodney (*faltering slightly*) What do you mean?

Mr Papadopoulos During the war. The First World War.

Rodney's facial tic starts up

Virginia (*rising to her feet*) Please don't remind him of the war, Mr Papadopoulos.

Rodney's facial tic becomes even more pronounced

Mr Papadopoulos (*continuing relentlessly*) In the trenches. In the cold, damp, muddy trenches.

Rodney backs away, gibbering incoherently

That was where you became a hero, wasn't it, Major Pirbright?

Rodney (*drawing his service revolver from his pocket*) What do you mean? What do you know, Mr Papadopoulos?

Mr Papadopoulos Oh, a great deal. Yes, I know a great deal, Major Pirbright.

Rodney About what?

Mr Papadopoulos (*taking his time*) About . . .

Virginia Stop it, Mr Papadopoulos! Stop torturing him!

Mr Papadopoulos About a dead man called Stukely-Pilkington.

Rodney (*horrified by the name*) No, no! (*He hurries to the door*) No, don't talk to me about Stukely-Pilkington!

Virginia (*rushing after him*) Rodney, it's all right!

Rodney (*putting the gun to his head*) No, no, I can't stand any more! Stukely-Pilkington! The dreams, the dreadful dreams!

Virginia Rodney, no!

She tries to wrestle the gun from his grasp. She pulls it away from him. When it is pointing at the drinks trolley the gun goes off. The newly filled decanter on the drinks trolley shatters

Tim Good God!

Boris (*leaping up on to the stage*) What the devil's going on?

Drawn by the sound of the shot, Renee and Christa appear at the french windows. Renee is holding a carving knife. Pat and Sophie enter DR

The whole cast is now onstage

Renee What happened?

Tim The gun must've had a live bullet in it.

Boris What! Harrison, I thought you checked it.

Harrison I did check it.

Boris Look, what is going on with this show? Someone could have been killed.

Harrison I'm sorry. I'm sure I only brought in the box of blanks.

Tim (*handing him the gun*) Well, clearly you didn't. Go and reload it.

Boris And this time make sure they're all blanks. God, Harrison, when I cast this show, I was worried about you being past it. I didn't know you were suffering from senile dementia!

Harrison (*recoiling as if stung by the insult, but then speaking in a subdued voice*) I'll go and check the gun again.

Harrison, crestfallen, exits L

Renee (*putting down her carving knife on the drinks trolley and looking at the mess*) So we're going to need another decanter, apart from anything else.

Boris Mm. Have we got one, Pat?

Pat (*picking an empty one up off the drinks trolley*) Yes. Got a set of them cheap in a car boot sale.

Boris Good. Go and fill it.

Pat is about to go off with the decanter

No, get that mess cleared up first.

Pat puts the decanter back down on the drinks trolley and crosses L

And hurry! We're getting hideously behind.

Pat (*a bit testily*) All right. (*She reaches round the corner of the* DL *proscenium arch and brings out a brush and dustpan. She goes across to sweep up the broken decanter*)

Sophie (*over this action, picking up the decanter*) I'll get this filled. Cold tea is it, Pat?

Pat Cold tea for whisky. Diluted apple juice for sherry.

Sophie OK.

Sophie exits L

Boris (*looking at a note on his clipboard*) Tim, your shell-shock routine was hideously over the top again.

Tim It's got to be over the top. The change of character is so psychologically unconvincing, you have to really hammer it to get it across.

Sophie comes back on stage without the decanter, but holding the portable phone

Sophie It's for—

Sophie sees that Boris is engaged in an argument and hands the phone to Pat. Boris's and Tim's argument continues uninterrupted by Sophie's and Pat's exchange

(*To Pat*) It's for Boris.

Sophie exits

Boris It is not psychologically unconvincing.

Tim Of course it is. "Murder at Priorswell Manor" is total crap and you know it.

Boris What I know is that it'll make a successful touring production. Anything with "murder" in the title, that's what the public wants.

Tim Used to want. You're out of touch, Boris.

Pat (*on the phone*) He'll just be a minute. What's that? (*She listens to what the person on the other end of the phone is saying*) Oh, really?

Boris (*over Pat's speech*) How dare you call me out of touch! Just because you aren't a good enough actor to—

Renee Please, can we stop this? I'm getting a headache. When we're ready to start again, you'll find me in my dressing room. (*She stalks majestically towards the* DR *exit, then stops for a moment*) Oh, and Christa, do come along. There's something I'd like to show you.

Christa (*following her*) Really?

Renee and Christa exit DR

Pat (*holding the portable phone towards Boris*) Phone call for you, Boris. From New York.

Boris (*taking the phone*) Oh, I'd better take it. I'll finish with you later, Tim.

Tim (*muttering as he stomps savagely off*) I'll finish with you the first opportunity I get, Boris!

Tim exits L

Boris (*on the phone*) Hello. Oh, Bob, hi. (*He props himself against the edge of the stage to take the call*)

Pat goes back to sweeping up the broken glass. Ginette is about to wander off L, *but Boris gestures to her to stay. She hovers near him*

Well, that's great news. (*He puts his hand over the receiver and whispers to Ginette*) Bob's cleared my appointment with his theatre board. (*Back on the phone*) Great. Yeah, well, I'll want to run the contract past my agent, but I don't foresee any problems. (*With a chuckle*) Well, yes, money, of course. There's always money. No, I'd be free next month—once I've got my current production up and running.

Ginette looks alarmed at this and moves forward a little. Boris reaches up and takes her hand to reassure her

And then there'll be someone joining me in the Big Apple a couple of months later.

Ginette smiles with relief

Great, Bob. Looking forward to it. 'Bye—missing you already. (*He presses a button to terminate the call and springs to his feet. Checking that Pat is turned away from them, he gives Ginette a little peck on the cheek)* See, my beautiful, I told you it was all going to happen. You'll take America by storm.

Ginette *(with a little giggle)* Oh.

Boris I mean it. Now I don't often say this to anyone, Ginette . . . but I really think you've got star quality.

Ginette simpers. Boris looks at his watch

Oh no! *(Calling off L)* Come on, you lot, we've got work to do! Where is everyone? Onstage, everyone.

Boris exits L, taking the portable phone with him. Ginette follows him

The stage is empty except for Pat, who is just finishing cleaning up the broken glass

Pat exits L with the dustpan and brush

Renee and Christa come on R: Renee looks smug, Christa shocked

Renee *(in a whisper)* Well, we all have secrets in our pasts, don't we?

Christa *(also in a whisper)* Where did you find it?

Renee Pure luck. Serendipity. I was browsing in a junk shop and I came across a pile of old magazines.

Christa But my name wouldn't have been on it.

Renee Not your current name, no. It was before the days of Christa d'Amato. When you were just plain Christine Briggs. But I recognised you. Apart from anything else, after sharing a dressing room with you, I recognised the moles.

Christa I was very young.

Renee Oh, yes, we all did work we're not that proud of when we were young. Mine never actually involved taking my clothes off, though.

Christa Where is the magazine now?

Renee Around the theatre somewhere. In a very safe place.

Christa And what are you proposing to do about it?

Renee *(casually)* Oh, I don't know. I'd have thought the photographs might interest the top brass at VOMIT, though.

Christa V*A*MIT.

Renee Of course. "Values and Morality in Television"——that's right, isn't it . . .?

Christa looks grim, but does not reply

No, I haven't decided what I'll do with them yet . . . Mind you, it'd

be a nice little item for the "Harley's Hotel" fan magazine,
wouldn't it?

Christa (*furious*) Renee, if you dare—

*Christa is stopped by the return of Boris, clapping his hands and
hurrying on Ginette, Harrison and Sophie. Pat follows, holding open the
prompt copy*

Boris OK, I want to go back on the scene we've just done.

Renee (*looking at the drinks trolley*) We still haven't got the new
decanter, Pat.

Pat Did you fill it, Sophie?

Sophie No, sorry. The phone went and I forgot.

Pat I'll get it in a minute, Renee.

Harrison Which scene is it we're doing, Boris, sorry?

Boris The one where you come in to Rodney and Virginia.

Christa Well, I'm not needed for that.

   Christa exits L

Sophie Surely you're needed just after—

But too late. Christa has gone

Harrison (*a little bemused*) Where I come in to Rodney and Virginia
did you say, Boris?

Boris The scene we've just done! For God's sake, Harrison, have you
got *any* short-term memory left? All right, let's do it.

Ginette We'll need Tim, won't we?

Boris (*shouting*) Of course we'll need Tim!

Sophie Keep your hair on, Boris. I'll go and get him.

   Sophie exits L

Ginette What was wrong with it, Boris? Any notes for me?

Boris No, you just do it the way you did last time.

*Boris turns to consult something in Pat's prompt copy. Renee sidles up to
Ginette with a patronising smile*

Renee Yes, remember, dear. Just like last time. The only way you can
do it.

   Sophie and a disgruntled-looking Tim enter L

Tim (*challenging the director to answer "yes"*) We're not doing the
shell-shock bit again, are we, Boris?

Boris (*deciding it isn't worth getting into another fight*) No. We'll take it from after Rodney and Virginia's exit. Mr Papadopoulos on his own, and you're about to enter, Renee.
Renee With Christa. Where is Christa?
Pat I'll get her.

Pat exits L

Harrison (*uncertain*) Right. So I'm centre stage—they've just gone off . . . Yes?
Boris Exactly. OK, clear the stage.

Tim, Ginette, Sophie and Boris step down into the auditorium

Just Harrison there. Renee standing by and . . . where's Christa?

Christa enters bad-temperedly L *and joins Renee by the french windows*

Christa I'm here.
Boris OK, and—
Christa Just a minute. Props. (*She picks up the carving knife from the drinks trolley and holds its point forward to Renee*)
Harrison (*amused*) Huh. You look as if you're about to stab her with the thing.
Christa (*turning a baleful eye on him*) Don't think I wouldn't like to.

Harrison gives a little chuckle, then realises she isn't joking. Christa hands the carving knife to Renee

Boris Can we get started, please?
Harrison Yes, of course, love. What's the line?
Boris (*bellowing offstage*) Pat, what's the line?

No response

She's not there. You'll have to . . . Oh, look, there isn't a line, for God's sake. You just watch them go out and laugh.
Harrison Oh yes, right.

Harrison stands C

Renee and Christa go out of sight through the french windows

Boris shouts at Tim and Sophie who are whispering in the auditorium

Boris Quiet. OK—and—action!

There is a silence. Harrison looks confused

Harrison Sorry. What do I do?

Boris You laugh, you idiot, you *laugh*!

Harrison Oh yes, of course. "Mr Papadopoulos lets out an evil laugh."

Boris Exactly.

Harrison (*after a pause*) Well, shall I let one out then?

Boris Yes, for God's sake! Let it out!

Mr Papadopoulos lets out an evil laugh. Then he looks around the room until he sees the desk. He goes across to it and, drawing a penknife out of his pocket, quickly breaks the lock. He takes out a sheaf of papers and is looking through them, when he hears a sound from the garden. He stuffs the papers in his inside pocket, gently closes the desk lid and looks around for a hiding place. His eyes light on the cupboard. He goes across, opens it and gets inside, pulling the doors closed behind him

Lady Dorothy Cholmondley and Mrs Puttock appear at the open french windows. Lady Dorothy is holding the large carving knife in front of her, rather in Lady Macbeth style

Mrs Puttock I must say, I still don't like the idea, milady.

Their conversation is continuous, but during Lady Dorothy's next speech, the doors of the cupboard concealing Mr Papadopoulos slowly swing open

Lady Dorothy Mrs Puttock, it's a matter of life and death. Unless we do something, a terrible crime is going to take place here at Priorswell Manor. Unless we answer evil with evil, there is a very real danger that . . . (*She becomes aware of the cupboard doors opening. As Renee*) Oh, for heaven's sake! I swear he's doing it deliberately!

Boris (*jumping up on the stage*) Pat! Pat, for God's sake! The bloody door still doesn't close properly!

There is a general confusion of chatter among the actors, out of which individual lines are heard

Harrison steps out of the cupboard

Renee (*rounding on Harrison*) You ridiculous old man! I will not work with someone who deliberately tries to sabotage my performance!

Christa Not that much there to sabotage, I'd have said.

Renee (*rounding on Christa*) And don't you start! You know I can get back at you any moment I want to !

Tim This is typical of the whole bloody shambles! What we need is a different director and a different show!

Harrison I'm frightfully sorry. I don't know how it happened. Reminds me, though, of a similar incident when I was working with Larry at Stratford in—

Boris (*imposing control*) Quiet! Quiet! QUIET!!! Pat, where the hell are you?

The cast are grudgingly silent

Pat enters L, holding the empty decanter

Pat What's the matter?

Boris Your precious door only came open again.

Pat Oh no.

Renee And haven't you filled that decanter yet?

Pat I was just about to when Boris called. I'll put it down and be with you in a sec.

Pat exits L with the decanter

Renee (*looking at the cupboard*) Something's got to be done about this. Once again it made complete nonsense of one of my most important entrances.

Pat enters L minus decanter

Pat All right, all right. Let's have a look at it. (*She goes to the cupboard and tests the door-catch*) It should've worked.

Renee See—I told you the old fool was doing it deliberately.

Harrison I wasn't!

Pat (*taking a screwdriver out of her pocket and starting to fiddle with the catch*) I may be able to sort this out. Otherwise I'll have to put another catch on.

Boris Well, we can't do that now. We'll have to move on. I want to have another go at the end of Act One.

Renee But we've got to do this bit again. It's not working. Don't you realise—I am trying to give a performance here!

Christa Keep at it. One day maybe you'll succeed.

Renee gives Christa a seething look

Boris I'm sorry, we must press on.

Renee You bastard! You don't care at all about me!

Boris Renee, my love!

Renee But don't worry—I'll get my own back on you. (*She moves statuesquely across the stage*) If I'm required, I'll be in my dressing room.

Renee stalks off R

There is a brief silence

Boris OK. I want to do the very end of Act One.

Tim Where from?

Boris Mrs Puttock's entrance—somewhere round there. Pat, who'll we need?

Pat (*still fiddling in the cupboard*) Lady Dorothy, Mrs Puttock, Rodney, Virginia and Mr Papadopoulos.

Boris Right, and, Harrison, remember, I want you really bloody.

Harrison Willco, old chap. (*Moving R*) I'll go and sort it out.

Boris I want to be shocked, mind—really shocked.

Harrison Do my best.

Harrison exits R

Boris Right now . . . what else?

Ginette Any notes for me on last time we did it?

Boris Just clarity for you, love. Make sure we hear all the little words—"if"s and "and"s and "but"s, you know.

Ginette All right, Boris.

Sophie giggles

Boris And, Tim, I think we might get more of a feeling of Rodney's instability if you take your voice into a higher register.

Tim Higher register? Squeaky, you mean?

Sophie giggles

Boris A bit. Try it.

Tim (*unenthusiastically*) If you say so. Where's the gun?

Pat I think Harry's still got it.

Tim I'll check what bullets he's put in. See if we can prevent the old loony from getting someone killed.

Tim exits R

Boris (*consulting his clipboard*) And, Christa . . .

Christa Hm?

Boris Make Mrs Puttock a bit older.

Christa (*surprised*) Older?

Boris Yes.

Sophie giggles

Christa (*shrugging*) If you say so.

Christa exits R

Boris Ooh, and I had a note for you, Sophie.

Sophie Mm?

Boris (*finding it*) That apron. It's too small. Makes you look like . . . I don't know . . .?

Sophie A French tart?

Boris A French tart, exactly. See if there's a bigger one in Wardrobe.

Sophie (*with a sexy little curtsy and giggle*) Oui, Monsieur.

Sophie exits R

Boris (*looking round the stage*) Now, is it all set? I'm going to do the lights for this, Pat. Got to check Harrison falls into the patch I told him to.

Pat (*with screws in her mouth*) Yes. Oh, we haven't got Renee's precious decanter. I'm tied up with this. Can you get it? It's in the Green Room.

Boris OK. (*Consulting his clipboard as he goes*) Now was there anything else?

Boris exits L

Ginette and Pat are alone on stage. Ginette moves tentatively towards the cupboard

Ginette (*with a little giggle*) Everyone a bit on tenterhooks, aren't they?

Pat (*preoccupied*) Hm?

Ginette Do you get nervous before a first night?

Pat No. I've done too many.

Ginette Ah, but not all with Boris.

Pat Most of them. Too many with Boris, that's for sure. (*She steps out of the cupboard and closes the doors. They stay closed*) There, done. (*She takes a list out of her pocket*) Just check the props are set.

Boris hurries back on, carrying his clipboard, but no decanter

Boris Oh, I've suddenly remembered. (*He goes across to a picture and adjusts it*) Getting a dreadful shadow from this. Meant to make a note, but I forgot.

Pat Did you get the decanter, Boris?

Boris Oh, damn, no.

Pat God, you're hopeless. Go and get it.

Boris (*assessing the angle of the picture*) Yes, just a minute.

Ginette (*eager to please*) I'll get it.

Ginette exits L

Pat is about to say something, but Ginette has already gone

Boris (*happy with the position of the picture*) That's right. (*Jumping off the stage and calling back to Pat as he strides down to the back of the auditorium*) I'll go and set the lights. Could you call the cast? Go as soon as we're ready.

Pat OK. (*She goes to the wings R and calls*) Could we have everyone for the end of Act One, please? (*She comes back on and looks round the set, making a final check that everything's in position*)

Tim enters R, holding the gun

Tim Well, I *think* the old fool's got the right bullets in it this time.

Renee, Christa and Sophie enter R. Sophie is wearing a bigger apron. Renee has an expression of intense concentration on her face

Christa Why on earth are you making that dreadful face, Renee dear?

Renee (*tight-lipped*) I'm getting into my part.

Christa Oh, how clever of you to get so much out of the subtext.

Renee What?

Christa I'd never realised before that Lady Dorothy was constipated.

Renee grimaces with annoyance, but says nothing

Ginette enters L, carrying a decanter containing what looks like sherry or apple juice. She goes to put it on the drinks trolley

Ginette (*to Pat*) Is that right?

Pat (*assenting*) Uhuh.

The stage lights start to alter to the setting they were in at the beginning of the play

Boris's Voice (*over tannoy*) OK, can you get into your positions for Mrs Puttock's entrance.

Renee drapes herself over the chaise longue

   Christa exits DSL

Sophie stands at the back by the drinks trolley. Tim and Ginette stand downstage

   Is Harrison there?

Harrison (*calling from behind the set*) I'm here, dear boy.

Boris's Voice (*over tannoy*) OK then . . . and go for it!

   Mrs Puttock enters, in distress, L

Mrs Puttock (*older than she was the first time round*) Oh, milady, milady!

Lady Dorothy What is it, Mrs Puttock? It must be something of considerable importance to justify the irruption of a cook/house-keeper into the library when my weekend houseguests are enjoying their preprandial—

They are interrupted by a huge thump of something being knocked over backstage

Harrison (*calling from behind the set*) Sorry!

Boris's Voice (*over tannoy*) Harrison, I am going to bloody kill you! I'm coming down!

Renee This is ridiculous. With all this stopping and starting, I just cannot act!

Christa Well, you said it, dear.

Boris (*bursting in from the back of the auditorium*) Harrison! You geriatric halfwit! What the hell do you think you're playing at! What on earth's got into you?

Renee Half a bottle of Scotch, I'd imagine.

Boris What? Harrison, have you been drinking?

Harrison (*from behind the set*) No, of course I haven't! I swear I haven't! Be all right this time—I promise.

Boris is now at the edge of the stage, from where he watches the rest of the action

Boris It'd better be. OK, from the same point. Mrs Puttock's entrance.

With bad grace, Christa once again stomps off through the DL *door*

And this time—make it good. Surprise me. Shock me—OK?
Renee OK.
Boris And—go!

Mrs Puttock enters, in distress, L

Mrs Puttock (*by now lacking only a zimmer frame*) Oh, milady, milady!
Lady Dorothy What is it, Mrs Puttock? It must be something of considerable importance to justify the irruption of a cook/housekeeper into the library when my weekend houseguests are enjoying their preprandial drinks.
Mrs Puttock It is of great importance. It's the carving knife, milady!
Lady Dorothy What about the carving knife?
Mrs Puttock It's gorn missing!
Lady Dorothy Gorn missing?
Mrs Puttock Yes, milady. And just after Sergeant Bovis from the village police station called to warn us there's an escaped prisoner on the loose.
Virginia (*over-emphasising the little words*) *An* escaped prisoner—oh, *how* too ghastly!
Rodney (*talking in a strange strangled high voice*) Don't worry yourself, my angel. I'll be here to protect you.

Lady Dorothy gives him a quizzical look

And you of course, Lady Cholmondley. Tell me, Mrs Puttock, for what crime was this escaped prisoner incarcerated?
Mrs Puttock (*dramatically*) Murder, Major Pirbright. Murder by stabbing.
Rodney Huh. (*He draws his service revolver from his trouser pocket*) Well, just let him try any of his little schemes at Priorswell Manor. He'll find that Major Rodney Pirbright is more than ready for him.
Lady Dorothy Major Pirbright, where did you get that gun?
Rodney From the war, Lady Cholmondley. (*His face goes into involuntary spasm*) Mind you, it wasn't the only thing I got from the war.
Virginia Rodney, please! *You* must *just* try *to* forget about *your* shell-shock.
Rodney (*nobly*) Yes, yes, my love. Sorry. Still, I'll just take a shufti in

the garden. (*He moves across to open the french windows*) Best to be
sure we're safe when there are ladies in the house.
Virginia *Oh*, Rodney, *you* are brave.
Mrs Puttock (*sobbing*) Milady, I'm so frightened.
Lady Dorothy Pull yourself together, Mrs Puttock, don't be
ridiculous. Triggs, my guests and I require more drinks. And, Mrs
Puttock, go back to the kitchen and pour yourself a large glass of
cooking sherry.

*Triggs, who has been standing rather bored at the back of the set, comes
to life. She moves forward, carrying a decanter of sherry, and refills
Lady Dorothy's glass*

Rodney (*looking offstage and continuing over Triggs's actions*) By
thunder, I think I see movement in the shrubbery!
Virginia *Oh*, don't shoot, Rodney! *You* know *I* can't stand bangs!
Rodney Sorry, my love, but you keep out of this. It's man's work. (*He
takes aim carefully*) And when the work required is shooting some
confounded malefactor, Rodney Pirbright's not the man to shirk
it! Right, take that, you delinquent scum! (*He pulls the trigger of his
revolver. It fires. He peers out into the garden*) I think I at least
winged the rotter.

*He moves back into the room. The other characters look expectantly
towards the french windows. Lady Dorothy gulps down her glass of
sherry. There is a pause*

*Mr Papadopoulos totters in through the french windows. He looks
very foreign and wears a rather flamboyant dinner suit with a jewelled
insignia on a sash across his ample frontage. His shirtfront is an
over-the-top gory splurge of red. He sways in the middle of the stage
area*

*Lady Dorothy is also having problems, clutching at her throat and
choking*

Virginia *Mr* Papadopoulos!
Mr Papadopoulos (*gasping feebly and dramatically*) I've . . . been . . .
murdered!

*He falls forward, face down. When he is on the ground the audience can
see the handle of a carving knife sticking out of his back*

The cast form an appalled tableau around him. Lady Dorothy, clutching her throat, slips from the chaise-longue on to the floor. She is suddenly still

The cast (except for Harrison), suddenly out of character, turn to look at Renee. Sophie rushes forward to her. She picks up an arm which falls limply. She listens to Renee's heart.

   Boris jumps up on stage. Pat appears from the wings L

Sophie (*turning to face Boris*) Boris . . . Renee's dead.

Black-out

CURTAIN

ACT II

Scene 1

The same. Six days later

The chaise-longue and the two armchairs have been turned round to face upstage, so that the audience cannot see who is sitting in them. UC *stands Detective Inspector Delver, looking the classic image of the plain clothes detective in a light raincoat over double-breasted suit and wearing a trilby hat pulled down over his eyes. He stands in a pool of light directed from above, so that his face is in shadow*

Inspector Delver is in fact played by Harrison, a typical example of Boris Smolensky's parsimonious casting. Because Mr Papadopoulos dies at the end of act one of "Murder at Priorswell Manor", doubling up the part with Delver, who doesn't arrive till Act Two, is a natural solution. For dramatic purposes, the audience should not immediately recognise who is playing the detective, which means that the actor playing Harrison needs to be heavily disguised with wig, etc. when he's playing Mr Papadopoulos in Act One. He should also aim for the maximum vocal difference between the three roles—Harrison, Mr Papadopoulos and Delver. And, for ease of costume change at the end of the scene, he should be wearing his raincoat over his Mr Papadopoulos gear

Delver You may wonder why I've called you all here into the library, and the answer can be given in one simple word. That word is . . . murder. Until only a few hours ago, a woman lived and breathed like the rest of us on this earth. Now she is dead. She breathes no more. A murderer has taken away her breath for ever. And that murderer took away her breath by one of the cruellest methods known to man—or to woman. I refer to poison—the means of killing favoured by cowards. As soon as I examined the poor woman's body, I knew the cause of her death. About her lips there

hung a bitter-sweet smell—which I recognised immediately as that
of a poison unknown to medical science. But have no fear, those of
you in this room who are innocent. I, Detective Inspector Delver,
will unmask the murderer—who I am confident is also in this
room—and bring him—or her—to face the ultimate penalty of the
law. The old rule of "a death for a death" may be thought by some
of a liberal conscience to be primitive, but in this case, I can assure
you, it will be nothing more than justice. So, murderer, hear my
words. Listen to what I say and tremble. (*Dramatically*) You will
soon be exposed like a hunted animal, because you have no hide to
wear.

*There is a silence, while Harrison realises he has got something wrong. A
giggle is heard from Christa on the chaise-longue. Sophie on one of the
armchairs echoes the giggle*

(*Recovering himself*) You have nowhere to hide. You will . . . You
will . . . You will be . . . (*But it's no good. The line has gone. He looks
hopefully towards the stage left prompt corner*) Prompt.
Pat (*off*) You will never escape . . .
Delver You will never escape . . .

A silence

Pat (*off*) . . . the majesty of British justice.
Delver . . . the majesty of British—
Boris's Voice (*over tannoy*) Stop, stop! The whole atmosphere's gone.
When are you going to learn the bloody lines, Harrison? I'm
coming down.

*The moody lighting changes to working lights covering the stage area.
Harrison looks shamefaced*

Harrison I knew the whole part when I went through it in my digs last
night.

*Tim rises from one of the armchairs. He is still dressed as Rodney
Pirbright, in military evening dress*

Tim That's a familiar line. Pity the others aren't equally familiar, eh,
Harry?
Harrison (*doggedly*) I did know them.

*Christa rises from the chaise-longue. She is now wearing the dress
Renee wore in Act One*

Christa Well, you're wasting time for all of us.

Harrison I'm sorry, Christa. I—

Christa And it's not as if you haven't been playing Delver from the start. The rest of us have suddenly had a whole lot of new lines to learn, and we're managing.

Harrison I know. I'm frightfully sorry.

Christa If I was still playing Mrs Puttock, I'd be safely poisoned by now and could be sitting comfortably in my dressing room with a glass of carrot juice.

Harrison That's hardly my fault. (*Calling off*) Pat, could I just have a look at the book, love?

Christa Any other director would have recast you by now, Harry. Only someone as mean as Boris would stick with you and save the cost of another actor.

Sophie rises from the other armchair. She is wearing the dress Ginette wore in Act One

Sophie Only someone as mean as Boris would manage to replace two of his cast without bringing in anyone else . . . (*She tugs at her dress, which doesn't fit very well*) . . . and put them in the same costumes.

Pat enters from the wings L. *She is holding the prompt copy, and is dressed in the Mrs Puttock costume worn by Christa in Act One. It doesn't sit easily on her, and she looks extremely disgruntled to be wearing it*

Harrison goes across to her to consult the prompt copy

Christa (*looking at Pat appraisingly*) And only someone as mean as Boris would draft in a Stage Manager with no acting ability whatsoever.

Pat (*glowering at Christa*) I've never claimed to be able to act. I hate doing it.

Christa (*going into a parody of an intense actress*) Yes, and it must be so difficult having the two roles of Mrs Puttock and Triggs combined. Absolute schizophrenia time for the kind of actress who really gets into her parts. I wonder how poor Renee would have coped. (*She laughs at the thought*)

The others look uncomfortable at this mention of the dead. To cover up the gaffe, Christa looks at her watch

What's Boris doing, for heaven's sake?

Tim Probably been waylaid by another reporter.

Christa Yes. He is taking an unhealthy relish in his role as grieving widower, isn't he? Seems totally transformed by the whole experience. (*Conspiratorially*) Maybe it really wasn't Ginette who killed Renee . . . Perhaps Boris did it, just to give him the opportunity to appear on the television news.

Sophie I doubt that.

Christa Oh, I'm not so sure. You know what'd really make Boris's joy complete?

Sophie What?

Christa To be asked to take part in a reconstruction of the murder for "Crimewatch." Boris playing himself—Renee and Ginette played by the usual actresses whose only previous work has been dandruff shampoo commercials.

Tim Christa, I don't think this is in very good taste.

Christa For heaven's sake, Tim. Stop being so po-faced about the whole thing. It'd be different if anyone had actually liked Renee. As it is, the world just contains one less self-centred bitch. Good news, I'd say.

Tim I was thinking of Ginette.

Christa Ah, well . . . She shouldn't have done it, should she? Naughty little girl. She should have known she could never escape . . . (*Going into an impersonation of Harrison as Delver*) "the majesty of British justice."

Tim I think you're being very insensitive.

Boris bursts in from the back of the auditorium

Boris Harrison, this is appalling! You're holding up the whole production! I delayed the opening by a week for the sake of the recast actors, not for you!

Harrison Sorry, Boris.

Boris (*jumping up on the stage*) Why the hell don't you know the lines?

Harrison They have been rewritten.

Boris About two of yours have been rewritten. Just because we eliminated the part of Triggs. Other people have had to learn whole scenes.

Christa Exactly. And, incidentally, Boris, we still haven't had that last rewritten scene you promised.

Boris I know, I know. You'll have it in the morning.

Christa I mean, of course I'm not worried about learning it. New half-hour script twice a week on "Harley's Hotel" and no problems at all, but I would like—

Boris It's in hand.

Harrison I will get that speech fixed, Boris, don't worry. Just had a look at it in the book and . . . Would you like to run the scene again?

Tim starts tapping his watch

Boris (*to all the cast*) No, I'd like to move on to . . . (*He sees Tim tapping his watch*) What the hell is it this time?

Tim Coffee break. Should have had one hours ago.

Boris (*exasperated*) Oh . . .!

Tim Look it's nearly six o'clock. We've been working solidly since lunch. Equity regulations state—

Boris Yes, yes, yes. All right. Ten minutes break. But no more than ten minutes—OK?

Pat Don't worry. The kettle's just boiled.

Pat leads the way off L. *Harrison, Tim, Christa and Sophie follow*

Boris Sophie, a quick word . . .

Sophie returns

Sophie Mm?

Boris Just wanted to say . . . your Virginia's coming together very well.

Sophie Oh, thank you.

Boris No, I'm getting to feel . . . you know, the person behind the character.

Sophie Good.

Boris Shouldn't really say it, but . . . you're doing the part a lot better than Ginette did.

Sophie Well . . .

Boris I mean, sweet girl and all that, Ginette, but . . . no great shakes as an actress, I'm afraid.

Sophie Ah.

Boris Whereas you . . . Now I don't often say this to anyone, Sophie . . . but I really think you've got star quality.

Sophie Oh. Well, thank you. By the way, Boris, have you been to see Ginette?

Boris What? What do you mean?

Sophie In prison. Tim's been to see her. I wondered if you had.

Boris No. I . . . It is very difficult for me, you must understand. Very complex emotions I have . . . you know, with Renee being dead . . . and Ginette having killed her. It takes quite a lot of coming to terms with.

Sophie I'm sure it does.

Boris I mean, to realise that I'm the kind of man who can inspire such intensely passionate feelings in a woman.

Sophie Yes, I suppose that's how you would see it.

Boris (*intimately*) Actually, Sophie, I would like to apologise to you.

Sophie What for?

Boris Well, during rehearsal, I have been pretty preoccupied . . . you know, I probably haven't paid as much attention to you as I should have done.

Sophie Hasn't worried me.

Boris No, but I'd like to make it up to you. Maybe we could have dinner together one evening after rehearsal . . .? Tonight maybe, if you—

Sophie Boris, I cannot believe I'm hearing this.

Boris What?

Sophie Less than a week ago your wife was murdered by your mistress, and here you are coming on to me.

Boris (*with injured innocence*) I'm not coming on to you. I just want to get to know you better. (*Playing for sympathy*) The last few days have been dreadful for me. I feel isolated, afraid I'll never again be able to make contact with another human being. I just thought that you and I could maybe talk and who knows what—

Sophie Forget it, Boris.

Boris (*accepting that his approach hasn't worked*) Oh. Oh well . . .

Tim enters L *with two cups of coffee*

Tim Call for you in the office, Boris.

Boris Ah?

Tim *Daily Mail* doing a feature on Fatal Love Triangles. They want a quote from you.

Boris (*very bouncy*) Oh, great. (*Realising that perhaps he sounds a little too bouncy*) Great, because if reading about my experiences can help some other poor tortured soul in similar circumstances, then Renee's death won't have been completely wasted . . . if you know what I mean . . .?

Sophie Oh yes, Boris. I know exactly what you mean.

Boris Ah.

With a quizzical look, not quite sure whether he's being sent up or not, Boris exits L

Tim (*handing Sophie a cup of coffee*) Got one for you.

Sophie Thanks. (*She takes a sip*) So . . . how was Ginette?

Tim (*with a rueful grimace*) Poor kid. Doesn't know what's hit her. Swears she's innocent. You know, Sophie, I'm sure she didn't kill Renee.

Sophie Everything points to her. She brought the paraquat in from the farm where she was staying. High-strength agricultural paraquat. And she told everyone she'd brought it for Renee.

Tim For Renee to use on her rosebeds.

Sophie Is that really likely?

Tim Boris had said Renee was interested in gardening, so Ginette brought her a present . . . as a kind of bridge-building exercise.

Sophie I don't think too many people are going to believe that in court.

Tim But it's true. I mean, I don't even think Ginette knew that paraquat could kill someone.

Sophie She must've done. Though she probably didn't know it would kill someone so quickly. She'd have been banking on the poison itself, not on shock. Unless of course Ginette was aware of Renee's history of heart trouble . . .

Tim I'm sure she wasn't.

Sophie Ironic, isn't it? Renee died as she had lived . . . by getting too deeply into her part. One good "Method Acting" gulp of her sherry and . . . bye, bye, Renee.

Tim Hm. (*Doggedly*) I'm still convinced Ginette's innocent.

Sophie Why? She'd got the motive—she knew she'd never really have Boris to herself while Renee was alive. And she was definitely the one who brought on the full decanter. We all saw her bring it on.

Tim But she didn't necessarily fill it.

Sophie Who else did then? The decanter was definitely empty when I took it off and got sidetracked by that phone call. It was still empty when Pat brought it on . . . you know, after Harry's cupboard doors had come open yet again . . . We all saw that, didn't we?

Tim Yes.

Sophie And then Pat put it backstage and was back on again in a matter of seconds. She certainly didn't have time to fill it then.

Tim No.

Sophie Then all of us went off to our dressing rooms, so the only people left onstage who could have got to the Green Room were Pat, Boris and Ginette. Since, apparently, neither Pat nor Boris left the stage . . . well, who is there left?

Tim Ginette still denies that she filled that decanter. She says it was already full when she picked it up in the Green Room.

Sophie But "she would say that, wouldn't she?". Sorry, you haven't convinced me, Tim.

Tim Listen, I'll tell you why I know Ginette didn't commit the murder.

Sophie Why?

Tim Because . . . and it hurts me to say this about someone I love, but I'm going to say it, anyway . . . Ginette's too stupid.

Sophie Ah.

Tim Ginette couldn't plan her way out of a paper bag.

Sophie You may have a point.

Tim I have got a point. Whoever killed Renee really thought it through. I mean, they may have only decided to do it on the spur of the moment, but they still worked out all the details of exactly how it was going to happen.

Sophie Mm. I'm still not convinced, Tim. The police seem absolutely certain it was Ginette, apart from anything else.

Tim Yes, but the police like the obvious, don't they? "Nothing like a nice open-and-shut case," that's what your boyfriend said, didn't he?

Sophie What do you mean—my boyfriend?

Tim That Detective Inspector Brewer. Seemed to be much more interested in investigating you than investigating the murder. He fancied you rotten, I could tell.

Sophie Oh, don't be silly, Tim. Bob's just—

Tim Bob, eh? So soon? No, he fancies you all right. (*Going into detective impersonation*) "But if you think of anything else, Miss Lawton, please don't hesitate to ring me on this number . . ."

Sophie Well . . .

Tim "Oh, and just in case there are any new developments you should know about, I'd better have your number too." Nice job, isn't it, being a copper—gives you the perfect excuse to ask for the phone number of any woman you fancy.

Sophie Tim . . .

Tim No, I don't think it'll be too long before you have a friendly phonecall from D.I. "Bob" Brewer, saying, yes, there has been a new development on the case . . . and maybe you two should meet up to talk about it . . . over a drink, perhaps . . . or might dinner be more convenient . . .?

Sophie (*embarrassed*) Come off it.

Tim (*reading her like a book*) I see. He's already been in touch. And have you met up with him yet?

Sophie Just for a drink.

Tim Oh?

Sophie (*still embarrassed*) He's taking me out for dinner after rehearsal tonight . . . assuming we finish at a reasonable hour.

Tim Well, well, well. So we have a tame policeman on our team, do we?

Sophie I don't know how tame.

Tim I'm sure you can get round him.

Sophie Even if I could, it'd take more than a few sweet nothings from me to make him change his mind about Ginette's guilt.

Tim What would it take then?

Sophie I'd say it would take solid evidence—or a confession—to prove that someone else did it.

Tim Well, that's what we'd better get hold of then, hadn't we? (*He lowers himself off the stage into the auditorium*) Come on, Sophie, you'll help, won't you?

Sophie (*also lowering herself off the stage*) All right, Tim. I'm with you. I'll give you all the help I can. Let's try and picture exactly what did happen that afternoon.

They both look at the stage with intense concentration, trying to revisualise what happened. There is silence while they do this

Harrison sneaks surreptitiously on L

Thinking he's alone, he checks around, then crosses towards the fireplace. He is just reaching up to the spray of weapons when Sophie coughs. Harrison jumps away like a scalded cat

Sophie Looking for something, Harry?

Harrison No, no. Just thought I, er . . . saw a cobweb earlier and was, er, removing it.

Sophie So nothing to do with looking for a bottle . . .?

Harrison Bottle? Good Lord, no. I'm off the booze these days.

Tim Completely?

Harrison Oh yes.

Sophie The other day, Harry . . . you know, the day Renee died . . .

Harrison Mm?

Sophie Just after the first decanter was smashed by the bullet, you were in the Green Room . . .

Harrison Was I?

Sophie Yes, and I came in. Carrying the new decanter.

Harrison Oh, I remember.

Sophie And I thought I saw you with a bottle then.

Harrison What? Oh, maybe I was—but that wasn't alcohol.

Sophie No? What was it then?

Harrison It was . . . erm . . . (*He realises he may have said something rather stupid*) That is . . . I mean, I don't mean that—

But further revelation is prevented by the return from stage left of Boris, Christa and Pat

Boris Right, let's get on with this rehearsal . . . (*Sarcastically*) . . . that is, if it's all right with our Equity representative . . .?

Tim It's fine.

Boris Good. Now I want to go back to Act One . . . that scene which starts with Lady Dorothy and Mrs Puttock . . . you know, and then Virginia comes in.

Christa The carving knife entrance?

Boris That's it. OK. And have we got that cupboard finally fixed, Pat?

Pat Should be all right. Put yet another catch on it.

Boris Well, I hope it holds. Seems to have a life of its own, that thing. (*He claps his hands*) All right, positions. Christa and Pat out of the french windows, Sophie off right, Harrison centre stage. (*He jumps off the stage to watch from the front of the auditorium*) The chairs are facing the wrong way, Pat.

Pat (*sarcastically*) So they are, Boris.

Pat starts to move them round. Tim and Sophie come up on stage and help her

Do you think that could possibly be because I haven't had a chance to move them round yet?

Boris (*not really listening*) Probably.

Pat raises her eyes to heaven. The chaise-longue and chairs are replaced as they were in Act One

    Sophie exits DR. *Tim wanders off left. Christa and Pat go out through the french windows*

Harrison moves centre stage and looks a little bemused

Harrison Yes, and, er . . . what's the line?
Boris Pat! Pat, what's the line?
Pat (*looking out through the french windows in a disgruntled manner*) Boris, I can't be Mrs Puttock *and* Triggs *and* be on the book all at the same time.
Boris All right, all right.
Sophie (*opening the* DR *door and poking her head through*) It's "Mr Papadopoulos lets out an evil laugh."
Harrison Oh yes, of course it is. Evil laugh—righty-ho.

Sophie closes the door behind her. Harrison stands C *about to let out an evil laugh, then suddenly stops*

    I say, I've suddenly realised, I'm in the wrong cozzie.
Boris Just let out an evil laugh, will you!
Harrison But it rather makes nonsense of the whole thing. I mean, Detective Inspector Delver'd never let out an evil laugh, while Mr Papadopoulos—
Boris Let out a bloody evil laugh!
Harrison Oh. Righty-ho.

Mr Papadopoulos lets out an evil laugh. Then he looks around the room until he sees the desk. He goes across to it and, drawing a penknife out of his pocket, quickly breaks the lock. He takes out a sheaf of papers and is looking through them, when he hears a sound from the garden. He stuffs the papers in his inside pocket, gently closes the desk lid and looks around for a hiding place. His eyes light on the cupboard. He goes across, opens it and gets inside, pulling the doors closed behind him

    Lady Dorothy Cholmondley and Mrs Puttock appear at the open french windows. Lady Dorothy is holding a large carving knife in front of her, rather in Lady Macbeth style

Pat acts Mrs Puttock very flatly, without animation

Mrs Puttock I must say, I still don't like the idea, milady.

Lady Dorothy Mrs Puttock, it's a matter of life and death. Unless we do something, a terrible crime is going to take place here at Priorswell Manor. Unless we answer evil with evil there is a very real danger that none of us will leave this house alive.

Mrs Puttock Oh, milady.

Boris Try and put a bit more life into it, Pat.

Pat (*turning on him ferociously*) I'm doing my best. You know I'm not a bloody actress!

Boris All right, all right.

Christa May I go on?

Boris Please.

Lady Dorothy (*indicating the carving knife*) I will hide this where we agreed.

Mrs Puttock (*over-emphasising the line with bad grace*) But, milady . . .

Lady Dorothy And you must go and get on with dinner. The guests mustn't notice anything untoward.

Mrs Puttock goes to the door L *then looks back pleadingly*

Go on, Mrs Puttock. It's our only hope.

Mrs Puttock nods, and exits

Lady Dorothy looks around surreptitiously, then moves across to the fireplace. She reaches up, as if about to slip the carving knife in amongst the other weapons. She hears a noise, and moves quickly to sit on the chaise-longue. She hides the carving knife behind her

Virginia enters through the door DR

Virginia Oh, Mummy, there you are. (*She sits beside her mother on the chaise-longue*) Rodney's just having a little lie-down before dinner.

Lady Dorothy A grown man having a lie-down in the middle of the afternoon? I must confess, Virginia dear, I do worry at the thought of you marrying someone with a sick mind.

Virginia Rodney's mind may be sick, but there's nothing wrong with his body. Besides, sickness can be cured. He's . . .

During the above speeches, slowly, inexorably, the cupboard doors have come open. Christa and Sophie stop as they realise this; the former is annoyed, the latter amused

Boris I don't bloody believe it! Pat, we're going to have to put a flaming lock on that cupboard.

Pat appears R

Pat It must be something Harry's done to it.
Harrison It isn't. I haven't touched the thing.
Boris Who's opening the doors then—a bloody poltergeist?

Tim enters L with the portable phone

Tim Boris, call for you.
Boris Tell them I'm in the middle of rehearsal.
Tim It's a journalist from the *Sun*.
Boris Oh.
Tim A *female* journalist from the *Sun*.
Boris Oh. (*Getting up on the stage*) Well, maybe I'd better have a word. Might be able to get a plug in for the show. All publicity helps. Take five. I'll be back as soon as I can.

Boris exits L

Pat I'm going to see if I can find a stronger catch for that door.

Pat follows Boris off

Tim (*on the phone*) He's just going to another phone. (*He switches the portable phone off and puts it down on the drinks trolley*) More coffee, anyone?
Harrison (*going across to Tim*) I'll come and have another.
Tim Ladies?

Christa shakes her head

Sophie No, thanks.

Tim and Harrison exit left

Christa So . . . I wonder how poor little Ginette's enjoying prison . . .? Let's hope it's teaching her the lesson that you can't go around murdering people and getting away with it.
Sophie She's only on remand. She hasn't been found guilty yet.
Christa Huh.
Sophie Christa, have you ever for a moment considered the possibility that someone other than Ginette might have killed Renee?

Christa No. Why should I? Ginette had a motive.

Sophie Other people might have had motives. Renee wasn't the most lovable person in the world.

Christa (*primly*) Take your word for it.

Sophie Oh, come on. She was always bitching at you.

Christa Yes, but someone in my position—someone who was seen by millions twice a week in "Harley's Hotel"—gets used to sniping from less famous actresses.

Sophie Of course. So you had nothing against Renee?

Christa Good Lord, no. If anything, I felt sorry for her.

Sophie And she didn't have anything against you?

Christa (*suspicious and, for a moment, unguarded*) What do you mean?

Sophie Just . . . (*A pause*) one thing interested me . . .

Christa Mm?

Sophie Immediately after Renee died . . . you know, after we'd phoned for the police and ambulance and everything . . .

Christa Yes?

Sophie I went up to my dressing room and I walked past yours . . . the one you shared with Renee . . . and through the crack in the door I saw you turning the place over . . . as if you were looking for something . . .

Christa Was I? I can't remember. (*Elaborately acting recollection*) Oh *yes*, I was looking for a scarf. Felt a bit chilly, so I was looking for my scarf.

Sophie I see. That would explain it.

Christa May I ask why we're talking about all this?

Sophie No particular reason. Just . . . a few people have been wondering whether it really was Ginette who killed Renee.

Christa Who else could it have been?

Sophie So far as I can work out, the only other people who could have done it—geographically at least—are Pat and Boris.

Christa Oh?

Sophie They were on stage with Ginette. All the rest of us were in our dressing rooms (*indicating right*) off that way. There's no way round the back of the stage to get at the Green Room, so . . .

Christa Mm. (*Pause*) Of course it is possible to get across under the stage.

Sophie Is it?

Christa Yes. There's a trap door in the wings. Haven't you noticed?

Sophie No.

Christa (*rising and crossing to open the door* R) Look. (*She points off*) There's a matching one stage left.

Sophie follows Christa

Sophie Oh, But you didn't see anyone using the trap door that afternoon, did you . . . you know, just before Renee died?

Christa Well . . . yes, I did, actually.

Sophie Who was it?

Christa Harry.

Sophie But—

Christa Now you will excuse me. I must go and top up my Vitamin C level.

Christa exits hurriedly R

Boris bounces back from the stage left entrance, looking very pleased with himself. Harrison, Tim and Pat drift on after Boris

Boris Well, that was most satisfactory. Sounds a very nice young lady.

Sophie The one from the *Sun*?

Boris Mm.

Sophie Did you do your interview on the phone?

Boris No, just a preliminary chat. We need more time to do it justice . . . all the emotions I am going through.

Sophie (*ironically*) Oh yes.

Boris (*avoiding her eye*) Going to meet for dinner after rehearsal.

Sophie and Tim exchange wry looks

(*Looking at his watch*) Right, so we'll just do one more bit, then break. I'd like to have another look at the summing-up scene.

Harrison What? Right back to "You may wonder why I've called you all here into the library" . . .?

Boris Bit later on . . . where you're going through the alibis.

Pat Will you be going back to earlier bits, Boris, or can I get out of this bloody costume?

Boris Why?

Pat Well, I'm dead now. Mrs Puttock's been poisoned and these aren't ideal clothes for touching up the paintwork in.

Boris Take your point. OK, you change.

Pat makes to go off ℝ

Oh, but can you just tidy that drinks trolley first?

*With bad grace, Pat stumps across to the drinks trolley and starts
tidying it*

As I say, I'm not doing much more rehearsal this afternoon,
anyway. Tomorrow's going to be a heavy day with the full
technical.

Sophie And one scene still not rewritten.

Boris You'll have the script for that in the morning, I promise. We'll
rehearse it first thing. At nine. I want you all ready to go at nine—in
costume.

Harrison Righty-ho.

Boris (*grabbing Harrison by the throat*) And knowing your lines!
Harrison, if you don't know every single one of them in the
morning, you're gone, you're out of the company!

Harrison But, if I wasn't here, who'd play my parts?

Boris I'd play your parts.

Harrison Oh. Oh. Actually, there's a rather amusing story of the
director taking over a part, when I was working at Stratford with
Richard Burton. He—

Boris Shut up!

Harrison, looking rather hurt, is silent

The chairs are facing the wrong way again, Pat.

Pat (*sarcastically*) Isn't that incredible? Must be something to do
with the fact that you've only just decided which scene you want to
do—and that you've just told me to tidy the bloody drinks trolley!

*Boris either does not notice or does not react to her sarcasm. Pat moves
away from the drinks trolley and starts to turn the chairs round, as at the
beginning of the act. Tim and Sophie help her*

Wouldn't think of giving a hand, would you, Boris?

Boris Of course not. I'm a director, not a stage manager.

Pat Huh.

*When the chairs are back in position, Pat goes grumpily off ℝ,
starting to remove her costume as she does so*

Harrison Actually, Boris . . .

Boris What?

Harrison Do you mind if, before we do this scene, I just glance at the lines for a moment . . .?

Boris That's wasting time.

Harrison Be quicker in the long run.

Boris Oh, all right. (*He looks at his watch*) I've got to make a phone call, anyway. Five minutes, Harrison.

Harrison Great. Thank you.

Harrison scuttles off L

Boris looks at his script

Sophie So you think we'll open all right the day after tomorrow, Boris?

Boris Oh yes, it'll come together. And we'll have good houses. All this publicity's really boosted the advance.

Tim And "Murder at Priorswell Manor" will become another nice little earner for Boris Smolensky Productions, will it?

Boris (*smugly*) I don't see why not.

Sophie And then . . . off to America.

Boris What? Oh, yes. Yes. Off to America.

Sophie On your own.

Boris Yes. On my own. It is sad, but . . . (*He doesn't sound that sad about it*) . . . there you go. (*He looks at his watch. Jauntily*) No, it's an ill wind . . . Just go and make this call, then we'll do that scene and break—OK?

Sophie Fine.

Tim And then dinner with your journalist . . .?

Boris Uhuh. (*He starts walking jauntily off* L) To talk about my sorrows.

Boris exits left, whistling

Sophie Not the traditional image of the bereaved husband, is he?

Tim No.

Sophie More like someone who's just had a huge weight lifted off his shoulders.

Tim Mm.

Sophie Two huge weights perhaps. Think about it. His wife's dead—his mistress is in prison for killing her—he can go to America with a clean slate.

Tim Start afresh.

Sophie I've heard of worse motives for murder.

Tim Do you really think . . .?

Sophie It's possible. Boris is certainly single-minded enough. And at his age this New York thing could be his last chance.

Tim But we don't have any proof?

Sophie Regrettably no.

Tim Well, I think the chances of someone like Boris making a confession are . . .

Sophie Let's say pretty slender.

Pat enters R, *dressed in her customary t-shirt, jeans and trainers*

Pat Can't tell you what a relief it is to get out of that bloody costume.

Sophie Pat . . .

Pat Mm?

Sophie You remember the day Renee died . . .?

Pat Hardly going to forget it in a hurry, am I?

Sophie No, of course not. Just before we all came back from our dressing rooms to rehearse that final scene . . . you and Boris were on stage—right?

Pat Right.

Sophie He says that you—you, Pat—didn't leave the stage before Ginette brought on the decanter.

Pat I didn't.

Sophie But what about Boris? Did he leave the stage during that time?

Pat looks evasive

Even for a brief moment? Come on, did he?

Pat I can't remember. (*Brusquely crossing* L) I must go and tidy up the props. There'll never be time tomorrow.

Pat exits L

Sophie looks at Tim in triumph

Sophie Well . . .

Tim Well . . .

Sophie Looking hopeful.

Tim Maybe. But any bright ideas on how we're going to get a confession?

Sophie Hm . . . You ever been in *Hamlet*, Tim?

Tim Gave my Rosencrantz once in Chelmsford. Or was it my

Guildenstern? God, even I can't remember. One of those twits,
anyway. Why, have you?

Sophie Did Ophelia once, yes. Modern dress production. Let me tell
you, it's not easy going mad in a T-shirt and cycling shorts.

Tim chuckles

Reason why I asked was . . . you remember? . . .?
    "I have heard
  That guilty creatures sitting at a play
  Have by the very cunning of the scene
  Been struck so to the soul that presently
  They have proclaimed their malefactions,
  For murder, though it have no tongue, will speak
  With most miraculous organ."
Do you get my drift?

Tim I get your drift, but I don't see how—

Sophie We still haven't had that rewritten scene, have we? If we were
to substitute something we'd written specially . . .

Tim You think our murderer might rise to a confession?

Sophie Might.

Tim But, even if he did, he'd never do a repeat performance for the
police.

Sophie No. So we'd have to have the police here. (*She picks up the
portable phone*)

Tim Your friendly neighbourhood Detective Inspector? Bob?

*Sophie nods. She presses the "on" button of the phone, is about to dial,
then stops when she hears something. She puts the phone to her ear and a
finger to her lips. Tim mimes "who?"*

Sophie (*whispering, with a hand over the receiver*) Boris on the office
phone. (*She listens intently for a moment. Then the conversation
apparently ends. With an air of triumph, she switches the phone off
and puts it down*)

Tim Something important?

Sophie Yes. I would say very important.

Tim Does it mean we're going to change our plan?

Sophie Oh no. Very much no.

Tim Still stick with the *Hamlet* scenario?

Sophie You bet. (*In a mannered Shakespearean whisper*)

"The play's the thing
That will the answer to 'whodunnit' bring!"
Tim But, Sophie, I don't—
Sophie (*looking off left*) Ssh!

They move away from each other

Boris comes bouncing in left, followed by Pat and Harrison

Boris Right. We'll just do this summing-up scene. Go and call
Christa, Pat.
Pat OK.

Pat exits R

Boris And you're sure you've got the lines, Harrison?
Harrison No problem. All shipshape and tickety-boo.
Boris They'd better be.

Christa and Pat enter R

Christa What's all this about a nine o'clock call tomorrow, Boris?
Boris It's to do with the new scene.
Christa But I'm hardly in the new scene.
Boris Nine o'clock! In costume! For everyone!

*Christa is about to remonstrate, but Boris doesn't give her time. He
jumps down into the auditorium and leans against the edge of the stage*

Right, in position, please, for D.I. Delver's summing-up.

*With bad grace, Christa goes to take her position on the chaise-longue.
Sophie and Tim sit on their chairs and Harrison stands* CS *facing them,
as at the beginning of the act*

Pat exits L

Harrison And where exactly are we going to start, old boy?
Boris (*consulting the script*) "You, Lady Dorothy, could not have
poisoned Mrs Puttock because . . ."
Harrison Ah, right. "You, Lady Dorothy, could not have poisoned
Mrs Puttock because . . ." (*Pause*) Erm, you couldn't just remind
me because *what* . . .?
Boris (*reading testily from the script*) ". . . because, due to your
allergy to cloves, you wouldn't have dared to touch the apple pie"!
Harrison Oh, right, yes. With you, old boy.

Boris OK. Go.

Delver (*moving menacingly towards Lady Dorothy*) You, Lady Dorothy, could not have poisoned Mrs Puttock because, due to your allergy to cloves, you wouldn't have dared to touch the apple pie. Nor could you have known that the top of the sauce bottle had an anti-clockwise thread.

Lady Dorothy gasps. Delver moves menacingly towards Rodney

So we come to you, Major Pirbright. You learnt plenty about poisons when you were developing lethal gases during the First World War, but did you have a motive? Did you know before this afternoon that Mrs Puttock was the mother of your half-brother Gervaise, and thus threatened to cut you out of Lord Godalming's will?

Rodney gasps. Delver moves menacingly towards Virginia

And then, of course, there's you . . . Lady Virginia. Butter wouldn't melt in your mouth, would it . . . but opium fumes would. Which is why you were discovered incapable in a low dive in Limehouse, accompanied by an enigmatic Chinaman.

Virginia gasps. Delver moves menacingly back to his central position

So . . . one of you three is our murderer—the murderer who not only poisoned Mrs Puttock, but who also stabbed Mr Papadopoulos. You know who you are—and now I know too. Unhesitatingly . . . (*He raises his pointing finger above his head*) . . . I point my finger at . . . (*There is a dramatic pause. It becomes too long to be merely dramatic*) Sorry, Boris, I've forgotten which one of them it is.

Boris (*a bellow of fury*) Harrison!!!

Black-out

<h2 style="text-align:center">SCENE 2</h2>

The next morning

The working lights come up after as brief a break as possible. The furniture on the set has been arranged back to its Act One position. The stage is empty. Harrison, dressed as Mr Papadopoulos, enters R, holding his copy of "Murder at Priorswell Manor." He looks surreptitiously around the stage, then once again homes in on the display of arms over the fireplace. He reaches up towards his hidden bottle. At this moment, Sophie, still wearing Virginia's evening dress, enters L she carries a blue folder

Sophie Goodness, Harry, those cobwebs breed and breed, don't they?

Harrison withdraws his hand and moves away from the fireplace the instant he hears her voice

Harrison Don't they just.

Sophie puts down her folder on a chair and moves resolutely up to the display of weapons. She reaches behind and produces Harrison's half-bottle of Scotch, which is now nearly empty

Sophie Not much left in this one, is there?
Harrison (*miserably*) No.
Sophie I don't know, Harry. It's almost as if you want your crimes to be found out.
Harrison Maybe I do. Some of them.
Sophie You're a stupid old fool. (*She puts the bottle back in its hiding place*) You could be a really good actor. Instead you're building up a reputation as being unreliable and "not so good after lunch."

Harrison looks miserably apologetic

So . . . any other little hiding places round the set?

Silently, Harrison goes across to the desk, opens a drawer and produces a half-bottle of Scotch. He puts it back, goes to the fireplace again, reaches up the chimney and produces another. He puts that one back in its hiding place

Real belt-and-braces man, aren't you? Any more?

Harrison shakes his head

Hm. (*She moves to the wings* R) Sure there aren't any more?
Harrison I don't know what you're talking about.
Sophie There's a trap door off here that leads down under the stage.
Harrison Oh, is there?
Sophie You know there is. Just before Renee died, Christa saw you coming out of that trap door.

Harrison (*guiltily*) She couldn't have done.

Sophie She did. So what were you doing down there, Harry?

Harrison I, er, I . . .

Sophie Were you just down there to have a swig from yet another hidden bottle?

Harrison What? Yes . . . Yes, that's exactly what I was doing.

But he still looks guilty. Sophie looks at him suspiciously

Anyway, why's Christa telling tales on me? A more relevant question might be why she was so interested in the trap door.

Sophie What do you mean?

Harrison When I was down there having a drink, I had the trap door closed. She actually opened it.

Sophie Oh.

Harrison As if she was about to go down. I can't believe she was just looking for me. I think she had a reason for wanting to cross the stage.

Sophie And are you sure you hadn't?

Sophie holds Harrison's stare. He is uneasy and moves across L to break away from her

Harrison There was one other hiding place I use for drink.

Harrison disappears into the wings UL

Sophie Oh yes?

Harrison reappears dragging a small wicker basket

Harrison It's this. Old props box, I think. Always lying about in the wings. (*He opens it, with the lid shielding its contents from the audience*) Full of all kinds of rubbish. The odd bottle just doesn't notice in here.

Sophie I bet it doesn't. (*She sees something in the basket*) Good heavens . . . (*She excitedly goes down on her knees to look in the basket*)

Harrison What?

Sophie (*excitedly*) There's something in there that—(*She hears someone approaching and rises to her feet*) Put it back.

Somewhat bewildered, Harrison takes the basket back off

As he does so, Sophie moves casually R

Pat enters DL. *She is dressed in her jeans and a different—though no less grubby—T-shirt*

Pat Morning.
Sophie Hi.

Harrison comes back

Harrison Good morning.
Pat Harry, I've had yet another go at those bloody cupboard doors.
Harrison Oh yes?
Pat Come and have a look.

Pat leads Harrison across to the cupboard and opens its doors. Sophie drifts downstage and sits on the chair where she put her file

There's a really strong lock on it now. When you get inside, you just click it across like that. And when you need to come out, click it back—yeah?
Harrison Should be able to manage that, old girl.

Over the end of this exchange, Tim, wearing Rodney's evening dress, saunters in R, *with a casual wave and "good morning" to Pat and Harrison*

He moves across to Sophie and speaks in a low voice

Tim All set?
Sophie (*with a nod towards her file*) Uhuh. It's even better than I thought.
Tim You've got something new?
Sophie And how! Something that turns the whole case on its head.
Tim What is it?
Sophie (*indicating the others*) Ssh. (*In an even lower whisper*) You know what to do with Boris?
Tim I'll see he's where we want him during the performance, yes. Is he in yet?
Sophie Haven't seen him.

Pat has finished showing Harrison how to work the cupboard doors. She wanders round the set, straightening pictures on the wall, adjusting the position of props, etc. Harrison continues to fiddle with the cupboard door, trying it out

Christa enters R, *in Lady Dorothy's evening dress. She is eating a stick of celery*

Christa Morning, everyone.

Sophie and others (*with varying degrees of enthusiasm*) Morning, etc.

Christa You should all have celery in the morning, you know. Lots of fibre. Really sends a message to the bowels that a new day is starting. (*She sits on the chaise-longue and takes a loud crunching bite of celery*) Do you know, I had sixteen letters this morning from "Harley's Hotel" fans.

Nobody seems that interested

They're getting up a petition to have the show brought back, you know. Going to write to the Prime Minister—see if he can make something happen.

Tim Well, there has to be a first time.

Christa gives him a cold stare, then looks round the stage

Christa So where's Ivan the Terrible?

Sophie Not in yet.

Christa Huh. Got a bloody nerve. (*Going into a cold Russian accent*) "Be ready to go sharp at nine—in costume!". (*She looks at her watch*) Well, we were ready. Where the hell's our precious director?

Boris enters L. He is extremely hungover and wearing dark glasses. He carries a blue folder like Sophie's

Christa And about time too!

Boris Please don't shout. I have such a head this morning.

Tim Good dinner with your little *Sun* journalist?

Boris Very good. They have big expense accounts, these newspapers.

Christa Well, I hope amidst all your carousing, you managed to do the missing rewrite. In case you'd forgotten, this show does open tomorrow night.

Boris (*indicating the folder*) Yes, yes, it's done. We'll do it straight away. Now the scene needs Lady Dorothy, Virginia . . .

Sophie And Mr Papadopoulos in the cupboard.

Boris Oh yes, right.

Pat (*slightly appealing for commendation*) I've done a new lock, Boris. It'll stay closed this time.

Boris I should bloody well hope so. (*He seems to see Pat for the first time that morning*) Why aren't you in costume?

Pat I thought I'd been murdered.

Boris No, no, this scene is before Mrs Puttock gets poisoned.

Pat Oh, I'm sorry. I get totally confused when I'm acting. When I'm
stage managing, I know exactly what's happening. Nature never
intended me to act, you know.

Boris Well, you're acting now—and I want you in that costume
immediately!

Pat stomps off R to get changed

Boris (*opening his file*) Now the new scene really hasn't changed
much. Just the odd line.

Sophie (*taking the file from him*) Shall I hand them round for you?

Boris If you would.

*He hands the file to Sophie. She goes across to near the chair where she
put down her file*

Tim You are doing this run with lights, aren't you?

Boris Yes, sure, I suppose I'd better. What've we got set at the
moment? (*He takes his sunglasses off and looks up at the working
lights. He winces*) Ooh. (*He puts his sunglasses back on again*) I'll go
up to the box. At least it's dark in there. (*He lowers himself gingerly
off the stage and starts off through the auditorium*)

Tim jumps down after him

Tim Boris, I wondered if I could just have a word?

Boris (*as he walks off through the auditorium*) So long as it's a quiet
word, you're welcome. Ooh, my head. You know, this girl, because
I was Russian, assumed I only drank vodka. Well, I couldn't spoil
her illusions, could I? She was obviously quite impressed with me,
you see, and . . .

Boris and Tim go out of the back of the auditorium

*During this action, Sophie has substituted her file for Boris's and handed
a copy of the stapled type-written sheets it contains to Christa, who
immediately starts reading*

Christa My bit doesn't look very different from the original.

Sophie Expect there are more changes later on . . . when Mrs Puttock
comes in.

Pat enters R, looking as unwilling as ever to be dressed as Mrs Puttock

And slap on cue, Mrs Puttock *does* come in.

Sophie hands a stapled copy of the new script to Pat

Pat Hope there's not a lot of changes.

The lights start to change, working lights giving way to early evening stage lighting. Only one of the interior lights, a standard lamp, is on, so the effect is subdued and dramatic

Boris's Voice (*on tannoy*) We'll go in just a minute.

Sophie Better get into position. Back in the cupboard, Harry.

Harrison (*looking up from his script*) What? Oh, right. (*He stands in the cupboard with the doors open*) Actually, I've got a rather amusing anecdote about some stage business with a cupboard. Happened when I was working with Edith Evans at the Adelphi and she had this scene—

Christa (*closing the cupboard doors on him without ceremony*) We're about to start.

Christa and Sophie sit on the chaise-longue

Pat goes through the door L from which she is about to enter as Mrs Puttock

Boris's Voice (*on tannoy*) Just a brief moment, then we'll be under way.

Sophie (*looking round the stage*) Where's Tim?

Tim's Voice (*on tannoy*) I'm up in the box with Boris.

Sophie Oh, right.

There is a moment's silence. Sophie and Christa—short-sightedly in Christa's case—peer up towards the box

Christa Do you want us to start?

Sophie Yes, Boris waved. Off we go.

The rewritten scene from "Murder at Priorswell Manor" begins. Sophie, Christa—and Pat, when she comes in—read their lines from the scripts. Sophie and Christa act the new lines pretty well, Pat less so

Lady Dorothy But, my dear Virginia, I had no idea there was any threat to Major Pirbright's fortune.

Virginia Apparently someone turned up in a gentleman's club in London claiming to be Rodney's elder half-brother, Gervaise.

Lady Dorothy But his elder half-brother was killed while prospecting for diamonds in the Amazon jungle.

Virginia Was *thought* to have been killed. His body was never found. The native guide told an elaborate story about trying to save Gervaise in some rapids, but it's thought he might have made that up in hopes of financial gain.

Lady Dorothy This is appalling!

Mrs Puttock enters DL

Ssh. Here comes Mrs Puttock. (*She rises to her feet*) You will excuse me, Mrs Puttock. I must go and check that Parsons has ironed the Times exactly as Mr Papadopoulos likes it.

Mrs Puttock (*with an inept curtsy*) Yes, milady.

Christa stops by the DR *door and peers up at the lighting box*

Christa So, is that it? I've only got one line changed. "Here comes Mrs Puttock", rather than "Here comes Triggs." I think I could have coped with that without a full rehearsal, Boris. (*Pause*) Why doesn't he say anything?

Sophie Because of his hangover. He's waving us on.

Christa peers up at the box, but her short sight does not enable her to verify this. She shrugs

Christa Well, thanks very much, Boris, for the nine o'clock call. Just what I need for changing "Triggs" to "Mrs Puttock". When I was doing "Harley's Hotel", we had whole scenes rewritten right up to the moment of recording—and I never dried once. (*Miffed by the lack of response*) If anyone needs me—for something more than a word change—I'll be in my dressing room liquidising some leeks.

Christa flounces off

Sophie peers up again towards the lighting box

Sophie He's gesturing us to go on.

Sophie goes back into the text before Pat has time to question this assertion

Mrs Puttock, there's something frightfully urgent I must talk to you about.

Mrs Puttock What's that, Lady Virginia?

Virginia Sit down and I'll tell you.

Mrs Puttock sits

Now listen, I want to talk to you about murder.

Mrs Puttock Murder?

Virginia A murder that took place a long time ago, but that may be relevant to what's happening this weekend at Priorswell Manor.

Mrs Puttock Good heavens!

Virginia It was a murder by poisoning. Someone put poison in a sherry decanter, and a woman died. There were a lot of suspects, but eventually the perpetrator was unmasked. It was the woman's husband who killed her.

Mrs Puttock Well, there's a dreadful thing.

Virginia Worse than that, he killed her and made it look as if his mistress had done the murder. He was a selfish and insensitive . . . (*She suddenly breaks out of character and looks up to what's happening in the lighting box*) What on earth's going on up there?

Pat What? (*Shading her eyes against the light*) I can't see.

Sophie It's Boris and . . . and that Inspector Brewer and . . . good heavens.

Pat What's happening?

Sophie (*calling out*) Tim! Tim, what's going on up there?

Tim's Voice (*on tannoy*) It's incredible.

Sophie What's incredible?

Tim's Voice (*on tannoy*) Boris has confessed!

Pat Confessed!

Tim's Voice (*on tannoy*) Confessed that it was he who killed Renee.

Sophie My God. Could you give us a bit more light, Tim? It's very dark down here.

The moody lighting changes to working lights. Sophie looks at Pat

Sophie You don't look very surprised. About Boris.

Pat No.

Sophie It's what you suspected?

Pat Yes.

Sophie It must have cost you something to say that . . .

Pat shrugs

. . . because you love him, don't you?

Pat (*looking round in embarrassment*) Well . . . In my way, I suppose, yes. I mean, I know he's totally unaware of me, but . . .

Sophie No one who didn't love Boris would take the kind of abuse you take from him.

Pat shrugs

Why do you think he did it?

Pat He had a chance of a new life in New York. I suppose he wanted to start with a clean slate.

Sophie And having his mistress arrested for the murder of his wife was an effective way of achieving that.

Pat nods

But now he won't be going to New York . . .

Pat No.

Sophie He'll be going to prison instead.

Pat Mm. (*She looks at her watch and moves to offstage with a long-suffering sigh*) I must ring round and find someone else to do the lights tonight.

Sophie Yes.

Pat goes offstage left

Sophie looks up towards the lighting gallery, gives a smile of complicity and a thumbs-up sign

Wonderful, Tim—it worked!

She goes off UR *and brings on the basket*

She kneels down to open the basket, again with its lid shielding the contents from the audience

Christa enters R

Christa What's happening? I thought we were meant to be rehearsing "Murder at Priorswell Manor"—or is that too much to ask?

Sophie Just having a brief break, Christa.

Christa (*making as if to go off again*) Oh . . .

Sophie Christa . . .

Christa Hm.

Sophie I wanted to talk to you, actually.

Christa (*coming back on*) About what?

Sophie About your rooting around in Renee's dressing room . . .

About your trying to go under the stage just before Renee died . . .

Christa (*looking guilty*) Oh.

Sophie I know what you were up to, Christa.

Christa (*petulantly defensive*) It's not my fault. If Renee hadn't been such a cow, I wouldn't have had to do it.

Sophie No.

There is a silence while the two women look at each other. Then Sophie draws a large brown envelope out of the basket

I think this is what you were looking for, isn't it?

Curious, Christa takes the envelope. She looks inside and, as soon as she sees the contents, clutches the envelope to her bosom

Christa You didn't look at it, did you?

Sophie (*reassuringly*) No, no, of course not.

Christa No. (*But the envelope seems to exert a powerful attraction for her. Cautiously she moves it away from her and peeks at the contents*) Oh, look at my figure. God, I was lovely when I was younger . . . just lovely. Do you know, men used to fall over themselves to . . .? (*She realises she's getting carried away*) Oh. Oh dear. Oh, I'm all of a . . . (*Overcome by emotion*) I think I'd better go and puree another parsnip.

Christa exits abruptly R

Pat enters L. *She carries a paint brush and a small pot of paint*

Pat I've managed to get someone for the lights. Suppose we should get on with rehearsing on our own, shouldn't we?

Sophie "The show must go on" . . .?

Pat That's it. (*She moves across to one of the downstage flats and starts touching up a cracked bit of paintwork*) Still, better do this first.

Sophie You don't seem very upset about Boris.

Pat (*with a shrug*) What can I do about it?

Sophie Do you know, I once heard Renee say, "The only way you keep hold of a man like Boris is by putting him under lock and key."

Pat does not respond

You'll enjoy all that prison visiting, won't you, Pat?

Pat I don't want it to be that way, but . . .

Sophie No, of course not. As a matter of interest, if for some reason *you* happened to be in prison . . . do you think he'd come and visit you?

Pat I assume you're joking.

Sophie So . . . if Boris hadn't been offered that job in New York, none of this would have happened.

Pat No.

Sophie He had the motive, he had the opportunity, Ginette was stupid enough for it to work . . . quite a neat little crime really. No, it all makes sense . . .

Pat Yes.

Sophie (*after a pause, suddenly*) . . . or it would do if Boris had ever been offered a job in New York.

Pat (*totally thrown*) What?

Sophie I heard part of a telephone call yesterday between Boris and an American actor friend. I talked to the actor later. He admitted Boris'd asked him to set up the calls. They were done just to impress Ginette. There never was any job in New York.

Pat (*in shock*) But there must have been. That was why Renee had to die.

Sophie Oh, I agree. It was. But if Boris wasn't going to New York, he had no reason to kill her.

Pat I don't understand. What do you think happened?

Sophie I'll tell you. It was an interesting crime . . . and it could only have been committed by Ginette or by Boris. None of the others of us could have done it. You couldn't have done it.

Pat Of course not.

Sophie We all saw you onstage with the empty decanter. You took it offstage, but were back within seconds. Certainly you didn't have time to fill it with paraquat then. And from that moment until Ginette brought the full decanter on, you remained onstage. So, as I said, you couldn't have done it, could you?

Pat No.

Sophie And if it wasn't Ginette, it must have been Boris.

Pat Doesn't seem any alternative.

Sophie That's the conclusion I'd reached . . . (*She suddenly goes to the basket and picks out of it an empty decanter*) . . . until I found this. So simple, really. I'd never thought of there being two decanters—even though I heard you say you'd got a set of them at a car boot sale. Here's the one we all saw and knew to be empty . . . before you hid it in this props basket when you went offstage. But of course you'd had plenty of time before that to fill the other one with paraquat and leave it in the Green Room ready to be brought on by someone else. (*Pause*) There . . . I think I've got everything pretty well right, don't you?

Pat (*bewildered*) So I needn't really have killed her.

Sophie No. I think you only decided to do it that morning, when you heard about the New York job. You'd coped with all kinds of humiliation from Boris, but you couldn't bear the thought of losing him forever . . . There was no way he was going to take *you* to New York, was there?

Pat (*bitterly*) No.

Sophie So you worked out your plan—poison Renee and make it look as if Boris was the murderer. That'd nail him down for you all right. What a pity that it was Ginette and not Boris who actually brought on the decanter.

Pat Yes. So what happens now?

Sophie Detective Inspector Brewer has been up in the box since we started talking. He's heard everything.

Pat Oh. And that business about Boris confessing . . .?

Sophie Tim and I set that up. Boris was waylaid by a telephone call. He doesn't know anything about any of this.

Pat (*calmly*) Ah. Well, if I walk through to the foyer, I dare say I'll meet Inspector Brewer, won't I?

Sophie Yes, I dare say you will.

Calmly Pat stands up. Suddenly she starts to tear off her apron and dress

Pat At least I'm not going to get arrested dressed in this lot. I'm a stage manager, not a bloody actress!

Under her costume Pat is revealed to be wearing her jeans and T-shirt. She leaves the Mrs Puttock clothes on the floor, drops down off the stage and walks slowly up the middle of the auditorium to the door at the back. Sophie watches her go. When Pat is about half-way to the doors to the foyer, they open

Boris and Tim enter

Boris Pat, come on! We've got to get on with this rehearsal. Move yourself!

Ignoring—hardly even seeing—Boris, Pat walks through into the foyer

Well, what the hell was all that about? Never mind. No, Tim, nice girl I've just been talking to.

Sophie Who's this, Boris?

Boris Got called away for another telephone interview. *Sunday Times*. Charming girl—terribly interested in me as a theatrical innovator.

Sophie Ah.   ) ᘔ

As Tim and Boris come up on stage, Sophie looks quizzically at Tim

Who was the journalist?

Tim Young actress I know. Very talented. Kept him conveniently out of the way.

Sophie nods and grins

Suddenly the doors at the back of the auditorium burst open, and Ginette bursts in. She is dressed in her normal clothes. She runs up the aisle

Ginette They've let me go! I'm free!

Boris What?

Tim Ginette?

Ginette (*climbing up on the stage*) The police are dropping all charges! That nice Inspector Brewer just told me . . . Isn't it wonderful news!

Tim It's terrific!

Boris I don't understand what's going on, but it's great!

Tim and Boris come forward from either side and give Ginette a simultaneous hug. After a moment, they realise the situation. Ginette looks from one to the other. The two men withdraw from the clinch and stand either side of her, looking a little awkward.

Tim I suppose, Ginette, it's time for you to make a decision between us.

Ginette (*after looking at each in turn*) I have made my decision. In my cold prison cell that decision was made. In future I am going to keep clear of all emotional entanglements. (*Nobly*) Instead, I am going to concentrate on my career as an actress.

Haughtily—even majestically—she swans off L

Sophie Oh, my God. That's all the theatre needs.

Tim runs off after Ginette

Tim But, Ginette! Ginette!

Boris Well, come on. Let's get this rehearsal going! We haven't got time to mess about! Pat! Where's Pat?

Sophie (*pointing down the auditorium*) She went that way, remember.

Boris Oh yes, of course. (*He jumps off the stage and hurries down the auditorium, shouting without sentimentality*) Pat! Come back! I need to start rehearsing! You know I can't do anything without you, Pat, you silly cow! (*Seeing someone as he goes through the door into the foyer*) Oh, hi, have you seen Pat?

Sophie hears Boris's last words and her attention is drawn by something at the back of the auditorium. A smile comes to her face

Sophie (*as she jumps off the stage*) Bob! It all worked! We did it!

She hurries delightedly through the auditorium

There is a silence on the empty stage. Then a tapping is heard from the cupboard

Harrison (*muffled*) Erm, I don't seem able to work this lock, Pat. Pat? Pat. Pat!

The tapping becomes a knocking. Slowly, inexorably, the cupboard topples forward and smashes down on to the stage

CURTAIN

FURNITURE AND PROPERTY LIST

ACT I

On stage: Spray of swords, pikes etc. on wall
Shield. *Behind it:* half bottle of Scotch
Drinks trolley. *On it:* bottles, decanters, soda siphons etc.
Cupboard
Desk. *In it:* sheafs of papers
Chaise-longue
2 high backed armchairs
Drinks table
Paintings etc.
Books
Standard lamps
Magazine
Sherry glass (**Lady Dorothy**)
Sherry glass (**Virginia**)
Glass of whisky and soda (**Rodney**)
Decanter (sugar glass) (**Triggs**)

Off stage: Hammer (**Pat**)
Stanley knife (**Pat**)
Modern sun glasses (**Christa**)
Container with creamy looking drink (**Christa**)
Portable phone (**Pat, Sophie**)
Sandwich (**Harrison**)
Tool box (**Pat**)
Cups of coffee (**Tim, Sophie**)
Plastic bottle full of yellowish liquid (**Ginette**)
Prompt copy of *Murder at Priorswell Manor* (**Pat**)
Carving knife (**Renee**)
Dustpan and brush (**Pat**)
Decanter (**Pat**)
Apron (**Sophie**)
Decanter full of sherry (**Ginette**)

Personal: **Mr Papadopoulos:** wig, sash with jewelled insignia, blood stain patch, mints,
penknife
Boris: clipboard with notes, script of *Murder at Priorswell Manor*
Pat: screwdriver, screws, props list
Rodney: service revolver

ACT II

SCENE 1

Strike: Coffee cups

Set: Turn chaise-longue and armchairs around to face up stage

Off stage: Prompt copy of *Murder at Priorswell Manor* (**Pat**)
             2 cups of coffee (**Tim**)
             Large carving knife (**Lady Dorothy**)
             Portable phone (**Tim**)
             Script of *Murder at Priorswell Manor* (**Boris**)

Personal: **Detective Inspector Delver:** raincoat, trilby hat, wig, other disguises
             Mr Papadopoulos: penknife

SCENE 2

Strike: Coffee cups

Set: Rearrange furniture to original positions
             In desk: half bottle of Scotch
             In chimney: half bottle of Scotch

Off stage: Wicker basket. *In it:* envelope containing photos, empty decanter (**Harrison, Sophie**)
             Stick of celery (**Christa**)
             Dark glasses (**Boris**)
             Blue folder *In it:* copy of fake *Priorswell* scene (**Sophie**)
             Blue folder *In it:* copy of new *Priorswell* scene
             Paint brush (**Pat**)
             Pot of paint (**Pat**)
             Script of *Murder at Priorswell Manor* (**Mr Papadopoulos**)

Personal: **Pat:** watch

LIGHTING PLOT

The stage of a theatre. Practical fittings required: standard lamps

ACT I

To open: Artificial, stagey effect with onstage standard lamps on

Cue 1	**Boris:** "End of Act One." *Abrupt lighting change to bright working light effect on full stage and small area to the front of auditorium*	(Page 4)
Cue 2	**Pat:** "Uhuh." *Change lighting to original setting*	(Page 34)

ACT II, Scene 1

To open: Artificial, stagey effect

Cue 1	**Boris:** ". . . lines Harrison? I'm coming down." *Change to bright working light effect*	(Page 40)
Cue 2	**Boris:** "Harrison!!!" *Black-out*	(Page 59)

ACT II, Scene 2

To open: Working light effect

Cue 1	**Pat:** "Hope there's not a lot of changes." *Working lights give way to early evening effect, subdued and dramatic. Only one standard lamp comes on*	(Page 65)
Cue 2	**Sophie:** "It's very dark down here." *Change to working lights*	(Page 67)

EFFECTS PLOT

ACT I

Cue 1   **Harrison** points the gun at **Boris** and fires   (Page 9)
Gunshot

Cue 2   **Virginia** wrestles with **Rodney** and the gun   (Page 24)
*Gunshot: Decanter shatters**

Cue 3   **Lady Dorothy:** ". . . houseguests are enjoying their
preprandial—"   (Page 35)
Huge thud backstage

Cue 4   **Rodney:** "Right, take that, you delinquent scum!"   (Page 37)
Gunshot

ACT II

No cues

For safety's sake the cupboard which falls over should be constructed with a false back
so the actor can escape before it falls

* In the original production the decanter was made of sugar glass and attached by an
"invisible" line to the wings. By pulling the line off stage the decanter was made to
topple over and shatter.